PUFF
RANI L.

Deepa Agarwal has written about forty books in English and Hindi, mostly for children. Among her recent titles are *Caravan to Tibet* (Puffin India), *Folktales of Uttarakhand* (CBT) and an English translation of *Chandrakanta* (Puffin India), the famous Hindi classic. A regular contributor to children's magazines, both in India and abroad, she has also edited and compiled a number of anthologies.

Deepa has received many prestigious national awards for her writing, including the NCERT National Award for Children's Literature for her book *Ashok's New Friends* (CBT), in 1992–93. Her book *Caravan to Tibet* was selected for the IBBY (International Board on Books for Young People) Honour List 2008 as the best book from India.

Deepa lives in Delhi with her businessman husband, and has three grown-up daughters and two grandchildren.

# Other books in the *Puffin Lives* series

Jawaharlal Nehru: The Jewel of India
*by* Aditi De
Ashoka: The Great and Compassionate King
*by* Subhadra Sen Gupta

# RANI

# Lakshmibai
## THE VALIANT
## QUEEN OF JHANSI

# DEEPA AGARWAL

**PUFFIN BOOKS**

PUFFIN BOOKS

USA | Canada | UK | Ireland | Australia
New Zealand | India | South Africa | China

Puffin Books is part of the Penguin Random House group of companies
whose addresses can be found at global.penguinrandomhouse.com

Published by Penguin Random House India Pvt. Ltd
7th Floor, Infinity Tower C, DLF Cyber City,
Gurgaon 122 002, Haryana, India

Penguin
Random House
India

First published in Puffin by Penguin Books India 2009

10 9 8 7 6 5 4 3 2

ISBN 9780143330844

Typeset in Bembo by Eleven Arts, New Delhi
Printed at Repro India Ltd, Navi Mumbai

www.penguinbooksindia.com

# Contents

*How valiantly, like a man fought she*
*She . . . the Rani of Jhansi!*
*On every parapet a gun she set,*
*Rained fires of hell,*
*How well, like a man fought she,*
*She . . . the Rani of Jhansi,*
*How valiantly and well!*

—Bundela folk song

# 1 ❊ I Will Ride Ten Elephants

The elephant obediently sank on its knees, responding to its mahout's commands. Three men mounted it— Dhondupant Nana Sahib, Pandurang Rao Sahib and Bala Sahib. The howdah was somewhat worn and the elephant hardly in its prime, but it was the only one the former Maratha ruler Peshwa Bajirao II owned, living in exile as he did in Bithur, close to Kanpur. The three were his adopted sons and Nana, his chosen heir.

A little girl came running up. 'Wait, I want to ride it too! I want to ride it too!' she clamoured. The men ignored her pointedly. She continued to cry out even as the elephant rose and padded off slowly. Her father Moropant pulled her away, frowning. 'You're the daughter of an ordinary man, child!' he said. 'It's not in your destiny to ride elephants.'

The girl's large eyes flashed. 'It's my destiny to ride ten. Wait and see, Baba!' Moropant Tambe just smiled sadly as he hoisted her on to his shoulder.

Some years later, this statement would come back to stun him, when he would realize that his daughter had possessed an uncanny sense of her own destiny. Manu, or Manikarnika as she was named, did grow up to ride many elephants—as Lakshmibai, the Rani of Jhansi.

At that time Moropant, a Brahmin, was employed by the Peshwa to supervise worship at his various shrines. Moropant's family had had a long connection with the Peshwas. His grandfather Krishnaji Anant Tambe had been a commander of the Maratha forces during the Third Battle of Panipat in 1761. When Peshwa Bajirao II was banished to Bithur by the British in 1817, Moropant's father Balwant Rao accompanied the Peshwa's youngest brother Chimnaji Appa to Varanasi and settled there, building a house at Assi Ghat on the banks of the Ganga.

Moropant grew up in the holy city and took over his father's position as adviser to Chimnaji Appa. He received a salary of about Rs 50 a month, a comfortable amount at that time. Manu was born here, to his wife Bhagirathi Bai. There is some confusion as to the actual date of her birth, but most sources place it around 1827. This might be a plausible date, because when Chimnaji Appa died in 1832, it is said that Manu was four at that time.

Moropant had moved to Bithur soon after Chimnaji Appa's death. But before that momentous move, the family suffered a tragic bereavement: Manu lost her mother when she was barely two.

Who knows how much the lively little girl missed her when she boarded the boat that carried them down the Ganga river to Bithur? It must have been exciting, no doubt, to go off on a journey so much longer than any she had experienced so far. Her father was already doing his best to fill the gap her mother had left, and the thrill of new sights and sounds probably occupied Manu's mind.

Life in Bithur was quite different from that in Varanasi. The old Peshwa had about 10,000 followers living there, so there was a large Maharastrian community. He developed a soft corner for the pretty little girl, so full of life, who ran around as she willed, unsupervised by a mother. He nicknamed her Chhabeeli, or the mynah bird, but when she grew older she protested on being addressed that way.

Legends are told about Manu's friendship with the Peshwa's chosen successor, Nana Sahib, who was much older than her, and Tantya Tope. It is said that they rode together and practised sword fencing and *mallkhamb*, a kind of gymnastics performed on an upright pole. Tantya was in the service of the Peshwa, a young man with a great interest in wrestling. Soon Manu became an accomplished horsewoman and also learned how to use arms. And, with time, she developed a relationship with the two, which was to have a deep influence on the course of events later.

Unlike many girls of her time Manu got an education—she learned to read and write, studied Sanskrit and picked up some Persian, the court language. She was also outspoken and independent. Since she had lost her mother, she did not have what is considered a conventional upbringing. There was no one to tutor her on what behaviour was suitable for a girl, and perhaps her father indulged her, too.

## Lakshmibai in literature

You might have learnt the famous Hindi poem *Jhansi ki Rani* by Subhadra Kumari Chauhan. It has greatly helped in creating the popular image of the queen as a fearless warrior. Often chosen for recitation in schools, it was inspired by a folk song.

Lakshmibai's life and exploits have featured in other literary works, too. Novels like *Jhansi ki Rani* written by well-known Hindi writer Vrindavanlal Verma added to the legend that Nana Sahib and Manu were playmates. Some say they were not close enough in age for that.

## 2 ✶ The Call of Destiny

As time passed, and Manu became a teenager, Moropant had to face reality. The custom was to marry off girls when they were as young as eight years old. Moropant was beginning to face a great deal of criticism for neglecting his responsibilities, when an extraordinary match practically fell into his lap. Manu was chosen to marry none less than Gangadhar Rao, the raja of Jhansi. She was fourteen at that time, while the bridegroom was much older. The wedding took place in 1842.

The kingdom of Jhansi lay in Bundelkhand, and the Chandela Rajputs had ruled there once, though their capital was at Orchha. When the Mughals began to dominate the country, they were in constant conflict with the Rajputs, who were occasionally compelled to pay taxes to them. But in Aurangzeb's time, Maharaja Chattrasal revolted against the Mughals and allied himself with the Marathas. After Peshwa Bajirao I supported him in battle against the Mughals, Chattrasal gave him one-third of his kingdom as a reward.

Jhansi lay in this territory. The subedars originally appointed were unable to control the region. Therefore one of the Peshwa's best generals, Raghunath Hari Newalkar, was sent from Pune to take charge in 1770. He was a capable administrator, but after ruling for thirty-four years, he had to abdicate the throne in favour of his brother Shivrao Bhau because of ill health.

In 1803, a treaty was signed between the East India Company and the Marathas. The East India Company acknowledged Shivrao as an independent ruler in 1804. After Shivrao passed away in 1816, his grandson Ramchandra Rao succeeded him. Ramchandra proved so loyal to the British that he lent them money for the Burmese war and provided grain for their troops. In return, they granted him the title of Maharajadhiraj Fidvi Badshah Jamjah Inglistan or 'Devoted Servant of the Glorious King of England' in 1832.

Ramchandra Rao even agreed to fly the British flag, which meant that they had authority over Jhansi and the king sat on the throne under their protection. After he passed away in 1835, his uncle Raghunath Rao took over. Unfortunately, he was incompetent and a spendthrift, and incurred huge debts. When he too died in 1838, without an heir, the British chose Shivrao's youngest son Gangadhar Rao to succeed him. Gangadhar obtained the crown after much wrangling between his stepbrothers and cousins, and opposition from his powerful stepmother Sakhubai.

The affairs of the kingdom were in a mess by now. Both his predecessors had mismanaged matters. Bandits roamed the countryside, and the local Bundela chiefs were creating havoc. It took Gangadhar some time to restore order, and with the help of the British, he finally managed to bring stability.

Jhansi had a population of 60,000 at that time. Carpet weaving and the manufacture of brassware and silk provided an occupation to many people. It was also an important centre for trade and distribution of goods, because of its location between the northern plains and central India. Once law and order was restored, commerce and industry began to flourish.

Gangadhar Rao had brought the kingdom back to its feet and gained the respect of his people, but he had no family. He had lost his first wife, Ramabai, and preoccupied with the affairs of state, he did not marry again for many years. There was, however, considerable anxiety about the fact that he had no son to succeed him. Hence he began to look for a second wife.

It was not easy to locate a suitable girl in his caste—especially one who possessed the qualities of a queen. He therefore decided to send trusted courtiers to different parts of the country to search for a bride. One of them, Tantya Dikshit, set off for Bithur, knowing that many Maharashtrians lived there. The Peshwa immediately suggested Manu.

Moropant was worried about his daughter, too, since she had passed what was considered a marriageable age at that time. He showed Manu's horoscope to the learned pandit. Tantya Dikshit's eyes grew wide as he pored over it. 'This girl was born to be a queen!' he said. 'Not just that, she is destined to bring immortal fame to her husband's family. Who is she?'

Moropant's heart beat wildly. 'Sh . . . She's my own daughter!' he stammered.

'Your daughter? I would like to meet her as soon as possible,' Tantya replied.

Manu was taken by surprise when she was asked to dress in her best to meet some visitors who had arrived from Jhansi. She guessed the reason, of course. Like any other young girl, she knew that sooner or later she would have to get married. The very thought filled her with anxiety, as she was not very sure if she wanted to leave her beloved Baba and the familiar life of the Peshwa's court and go to live with some unknown family. All the same, she faced the visitor confidently.

Her self-assurance and her bright, charming face made a strong impression on the courtier. When Manu left the room, Tantya Dikshit told Moropant, 'On behalf of Gangadhar Rao, the king of Jhansi, I'd like to ask for your daughter's hand in marriage. But I will have to wait for his majesty's formal approval.'

The match was grand beyond Moropant's wildest dreams. Bajirao had already vouched for Manu's lineage and character. Right away Tantya Dikshit left for Jhansi to inform his ruler of his mission's success. When he heard about Manu's extraordinary qualities, Gangadhar Rao immediately agreed.

The engagement took place in Bithur. Gangadhar Rao sent gifts of fabulous jewellery, expensive silk saris, a vast variety of sweets and dried fruit. As was the custom, he did not come personally for the ceremony. Manu now began to get used to the idea that she was going to be a queen. Another factor made her exult inwardly: she had heard that there were many impressive elephants in Gangadhar Rao's stable.

## Something about Jhansi

The city of Jhansi lies in Bundelkhand, a region in Uttar Pradesh. It is named after the Bundelas, who occupied this area in the 14th century BC. A Rajput clan, they ruled over several states in central India. According to legend, King Virsingh Dev of Orchha, famous for slaying Akbar's favourite Abul Fazl in battle, gave Jhansi its name. He had grown old and was losing his eyesight. When he looked at the city from Datia, a nearby fort, he said all he could see was *jhain-si* (like a mist). This description captured people's imagination so much that the name stuck.

# 3 ✻ A Royal Wedding

It was decided that the ceremony be held in Jhansi because there was no way Moropant could bear the expense of a royal wedding. Hence some of Bajirao's close retainers were dispatched to make the preliminary arrangements. It is said that Tantya Tope was also one of them.

When the time arrived, Manu set off for Jhansi, seated in the magnificent palanquin that had been sent for her, escorted by a troop of horsemen. Her father accompanied her, along with some relatives and friends. Occasionally, she peeped out from between the silken curtains to gaze at the landscape. It was the month of Baisakh, when the harvest is gathered, and farmers were busy in their fields. Closer to Jhansi the region turned far more rugged than the gentle plains she had grown up in. Steep hills broke up the smoothness of the landscape, with dense forests surrounding their bases.

When she entered the city at the auspicious time carefully selected by the astrologers, she was thrilled to see the huge imposing gates decorated with garlands of flowers and leaves, and the brightly-lit streets. All this had been arranged to welcome *her*—little Manu! It hit her hard—almost took her breath away—that this is what it meant to be a queen!

An imposing haveli, known as Kothi Kuan, had been chosen for the bride's party to stay in. It was furnished more luxuriously than any house Manu had ever seen. She was dying to run out and explore the city, which would be her future home. But an aunt, one of the many female relatives who accompanied them, said, 'You'll have enough time later, child. Right now it's important to behave decorously, else people will say your Baba did not bring you up properly.'

That was the last thing Manu wanted, that people should cast aspersions on her beloved father. So she contented herself with peeping out of the window to see the sights. Suddenly the sound of soft footsteps behind her made her turn. It was an attractive young girl, around her own age.

'I'm Sundar,' she said, bowing low. 'I have been chosen to serve you, your majesty. I will take care of whatever you might need.'

The gregarious Manu, who had been starving for some company of her own age, smiled and said, 'You will be my friend, not my servant.' Two other girls were close behind. They introduced themselves as Mandar and Kashi. Soon Manu was cross-questioning them about life in Jhansi. They told her about the king and the palace, even though she deliberately reined in her curiosity about the man she was to wed.

Manu was to be married on the full moon day. But she first set eyes on her future husband on the day of the Ganesh puja when he made his way to the temple for the preliminary ceremonies. The sight of the middle-aged man with a slight paunch was not that much of a shock since she had already been told that he was much older than her. She was pleased to note that he sat well on his horse. She also observed that he acknowledged people's greetings with the gracious air of a ruler.

As Manu waited in the house, bursting with curiosity about the city and its ways, strains of music wafted to her ears, along with chants of the priests.

'His majesty is very fond of music,' Mandar said softly.

'I have heard,' Manu replied absently, 'and theatre too, I believe.' The three young girls nodded vigorously. Manu suddenly felt disoriented. All this was so far removed from her former life!

It seemed that time was speeding as fast as one of her favourite mounts. When a group of lavishly attired women arrived to help her aunts dress her as a bride, Manu's pulse quickened with unbearable excitement. She was dressed in a silk sari resplendent with zari work. Magnificent ornaments made of gold, diamonds, rubies and pearls bedecked her neck and ears, and diamond bangles were slipped on to her wrists, along with the green glass ones that Marathi women were expected to wear after their wedding. An ornate nose ring studded with gleaming gems added its lustre to her large eyes. Her palms and feet were decorated with red lac, and toe rings and anklets of gold were placed on them, as befitted a queen. Fragrant flowers lent their charm to her thick, long hair. Then she was led to the place where the ceremony would be held.

The wedding rites stretched on within a gorgeously decorated mandap. Despite the overwhelming splendour of her surroundings, young Manu did not lose her self-possession. Even the solemnity of the rituals could not subdue her. When the old pandit's hands shook as he performed the ritual of tying her sari to the king's shoulder-cloth—to symbolize that they were now joined in marriage—she shocked everyone, including Gangadhar Rao, by calling out in a ringing voice, 'Panditji, make sure the knot is tied tightly!'

This incident immediately made it clear to all that the new queen was no conventional bride, timid and shy.

The festivities continued both in the palace and the streets of Jhansi. A hundred-gun salute thundered over the city when Ghulam Ghaus, Gangadhar's chief gunner, let off four cannons that rested on the towers of the Jhansi Fort. Manu had learned that they were named Ghanagarj, Arjun, Naldar and Bhawani Shankar. A host of important personalities attended the wedding—from the English Superintendent Ross to the rulers of the neighbouring kingdoms of Orchha and Datia. At the special durbar that followed the wedding, people offered gifts and received them in return. Food and clothing were distributed to the poor, while the Brahmins feasted on traditional delicacies like puranpuri and shrikhand.

## The Rani's friends

Lakshmibai's companions, Mandar, Kashi, Juhi, Motibai and Jhalkari Korin are inseparable from her in history and legend as they were in real life. They were her loyal confidantes, and fought bravely along with her. Some, like Jhalkari, have become celebrated as Dalit icons. While a lot of information about these women has come from oral accounts, they have also been mentioned in books like *Majha Pravas* by Vishnu Godse, a Brahmin present in Jhansi when it was besieged by the British.

# 4 🗡 The Queen of Jhansi— Lakshmibai

According to custom, Manu's name had been changed to Lakshmibai during the course of the ceremony. Mahalakshmi was the family deity of the rulers of Jhansi, and a magnificent temple was dedicated to her. A special puja was performed to bring good fortune to the newlyweds.

Gangadhar's occasional sternness did not cow down the irrepressible Manu, who was now getting used to her new name. After the celebrations were over, she began to discover what being a wife and a queen meant, especially the duties and responsibilities that accompanied this high position. She could not run around freely and had to mostly remain in purdah. This made her restless. Luckily she was able to convince her husband to let her continue the physical activity she was used to—riding, fencing and other exercises. It was hard for him to imagine a woman being so eager to pursue such sports, but eventually he agreed.

The Khas Mahal, in which they lived, lay within the fort. It was beautifully constructed and richly furnished. There was a garden around it, beyond which lay a parade ground surrounded with trees. Lakshmibai decided that this was an ideal place for her to continue her fitness routine within the confines of the palace. She did not exercise alone; she, in fact, drew her entire retinue of women into it. Soon they learned to ride proficiently and acquired all the skills she already possessed. One cannot help wondering if this obsession arose from some instinct that warned her of the trials that lay ahead.

Tradition demanded that she gain knowledge of the culinary arts, the different religious rituals and the correct ways to perform them. Her husband was keen that she should acquire learning, too, and hence put her in charge of the library. Lakshmibai took on all her duties with zest. It is said that a pocket edition of the Bhagwad Gita was her favourite book.

These responsibilities meant that Manu had to grow up almost overnight. The vivacious young girl became quieter and more thoughtful. The tomboy learned to clamp down on her quick temper and pick up the gracious ways of a queen.

Soon Gangadhar Rao invited her father to settle down in Jhansi, and provided him with a stipend for his support. Moropant built a Krishna temple there and maintained it as its priest. Since he was only thirty-two at the time, he decided to remarry. Lakshmibai's stepmother Chimabai was just a few months older than her, and the two developed a friendly relationship. Later, it was Chimabai's grandson Govinda Chintamani Tambe who provided much of the information about the Rani's personal habits to biographers. He had heard much about the 'Bai Sahiba' from his grandmother.

It seems Lakshmibai was particular about being neatly dressed and always polite in her behaviour. After the festival of Gauri puja, she would celebrate the women's rite of 'haldi-kumkum' or turmeric and vermilion, during which flowers and coloured powder were exchanged. She also invited women from the city to take part in it. On special occasions, she served her husband herself, though most of the time they ate separately, according to custom. People who had met her, like the lawyer John Lang who advised her when the British annexed Jhansi, have left accounts of her appearance. She had a round face and what is described as a 'wheat coloured' complexion, with a pleasing and intelligent expression. Her eyes were large and particularly striking, her nose finely shaped, and she had small, perfect teeth. Of medium height with a well-proportioned figure, she had a dignified bearing, which left a mark on all who met her. While her husband was alive, she was always splendidly bedecked in queenly ornaments—a jewelled choker around her neck, a seven-stringed pearl necklace and an elaborate nose ring, along with ornate bangles and anklets. She wore a sari tucked in between her legs in the Maharastrian style, and was especially fond of the delicate weaves of Chanderi.

Life proceeded pleasantly for the newly-weds. Despite the differences of age, temperament and tastes, they were able to build up a good relationship. Even affairs of the state had improved markedly.

When the British acknowledged Gangadhar Rao as the ruler of Jhansi in 1838, the country was severely in debt. The erstwhile ruler Raghunath Rao reigned for barely three years, and his predecessor, Ramchandra Rao, had faced many problems from his Rajput neighbours and lost much of his territory to them. Conditions became so bad that Ramchandra was compelled to borrow huge amounts of money from not only the British but the kings of Gwalior and Orchha. For this reason, in effect, the British Superintendent Ross actually governed Jhansi while Gangadhar simply received an allowance. Still, he tried to be involved in the affairs of the state as much as possible, and Ross was sympathetic.

Soon after Gangadhar Rao's marriage to Lakshmibai in 1843, the British decided to hand over the reins of the government to the king. However, there was a condition—he was to maintain a British battalion as a defence against possible trouble from the Bundelas and Rajputs. The people were happy and felt that the new queen had brought them luck. Little by little Gangadhar was also paying off his debts.

An elaborate durbar was held to celebrate the investiture. Huge drums were beaten and gun salutes given while the king ascended the throne to the chanting of mantras. To mark this phase of prosperity and good fortune, Gangadhar made many improvements to the city and built a magnificent four-storey palace in the Bundelkhand style. Its walls were decorated with beautiful paintings. The stone balconies and pillars were engraved with pairs of swans, fish and peacocks. This palace was lavishly furnished, too, with silk and velvet hangings.

According to an account left by J.H. Sylvester, a veterinary surgeon: *Its ceiling was of plate glass mirrors, the panels of the walls carved and gilded, and also covered by mirrors and paintings. The floor was covered with one huge cushion of cotton wool covered in crimson velvet, and one felt it was a sin to drag one's spur armed heels over it. The state room was also beautiful and lighted by four spacious windows. Its floor was covered by English carpets and Persian rugs; huge glass chandeliers, chiefly purple in colour, hung from the ceiling. Chairs, tables, couches, pictures and ornaments were abundant. The sleeping rooms, fitted up by one no novice in luxuries, were handsomely decorated after the Eastern fashion, scarlet and gold prevailing. The shallow bedsteads, scarce a foot from the floor, were of solid silver, their pillows and coverlets of gaudy satin and kinkob.*

Gangadhar Rao was deeply interested in the arts. He was fond of classical music, theatre and Sanskrit literature. His library was full of rare manuscripts. He personally supervised the royal theatre and saw to it that the costumes of the actresses were well designed. Occasionally he even took part in the performances. Motibai was one of the famous actresses of his time, and Mughal Khan an accomplished classical singer. Gangadhar Rao was thus famous as a patron, and many talented craftsmen and performers headed towards Jhansi.

All this was new and strange for Lakshmibai, who would usually refuse to attend the performances, saying, 'I am not interested in make-believe. Real life is more important to me.'

'And what is real life?' her husband would ask.

'The welfare of our people, the proper government of our kingdom,' she would reply.

It is said that when the king saw where Lakshmibai's interests lay, he left much of the work of the state to her and became more involved in the pursuit of the arts. It worked better for the kingdom. He was autocratic by temperament and handed out severe punishments to those who displeased him. Lakshmibai tempered his harshness and did not hesitate to speak out when she felt injustice was being done. She became known as a queen who lent a kind ear to supplicants and helped the needy.

Gangadhar once decided to gift a gorgeous silver palanquin to her. Made to order in Varanasi, he designed it himself. It was lined with red velvet cushions embellished with fine gold embroidery and golden tassels. The curtains were richly decorated, too. Whenever Lakshmibai would ride on it on her way to the Mahalakshmi temple at important festivals, people would stand still on the streets and watch.

Among his elephants, Gangadhar had a favourite named Siddhabaksh. Like any king's favourite, it was pampered and given sugar cane and jalebis to eat every day. Lakshmibai would sometimes feed it herself. The king mounted Siddhabaksh and went in processions through the streets on major festivals. Gangadhar owned another elephant with huge tusks. When the elephants paraded the city on such occasions, they were decorated with chandeliers and people marvelled at the spectacle.

### Turmeric and vermilion

The haldi-kumkum ceremony is a social gathering popular in western Indian states like Maharashtra. Married women exchange haldi (turmeric) and kumkum (vermilion powder), which symbolize their marital status, and pray for the long life of their husbands. Lakshmibai used this festival to bond with the women of Jhansi. Later, when the threat of a British attack began to create panic, she celebrated it in great style to reassure the citizens that life was normal in the city and they had nothing to fear.

# 5 ❋ Gathering Clouds

Life was not perfect, however. There were pinpricks from the British, off and on. Like other rulers, Gangadhar Rao was conscious of the growing influence of this foreign power, which was trying to impose its laws and customs into his country. There was also the knotty question of an heir for the throne of Jhansi. Nine years had passed since their marriage and the queen had not yet conceived. This was cause for great concern.

Gangadhar Rao decided to go on a pilgrimage to various holy places to seek the blessings of the gods. In early 1850, the royal party left for Varanasi. It is said that, along with a visit to the Vishwanath temple and the ghats of the Ganga river, the queen went to the house of her birth. An unpleasant incident took place at a reception organized by the British commissioner. A prominent citizen of Varanasi, Rajendra Mitra, did not stand up to greet the king. Slighted, Gangadhar had him soundly beaten.

They went on to Gaya, to perform rituals for the souls of their ancestors, and then proceeded to the holy city of Prayag to take a dip at the confluence of the three rivers—Ganga, Jamuna and the invisible Saraswati. The king had wanted to travel to Puri as well, but by chance Lakshmibai became pregnant. So it was considered more advisable to return home. They entered the city in procession: the queen seated on Siddhabaksh, with other elephants and mounted bodyguards following. The people crowded the streets and gave them a rousing welcome.

The whole kingdom rejoiced when Lakshmibai gave birth to a son in early 1851. Fireworks were set off and gifts distributed. Temples received donations, and ceremonies were performed for the welfare of the child and his mother. But sadly, baby Damodar Rao passed away when he was only three months old.

Gangadhar Rao was totally shattered. It was as if he had nothing to live for any longer. The loss was such a severe blow that it affected his physical condition. Little by little his health deteriorated and he started neglecting himself. Being a deeply religious man, he insisted on fasting during Navaratri, in September 1853, and went on foot to the Mahalakshmi temple to pray. The Rani and her father tried to dissuade him, but to no avail.

In that part of the country, at Dussehra, rulers observed a certain ritual described as 'crossing the border'. They would cross over to the adjoining kingdom and come back after a celebratory picnic. Gangadhar Rao was adamant about this, too, and crossed over to the kingdom of Datia. His weakened frame could not stand up to the strain of the journey, and he became so ill that he had to be carried back in a palanquin. The vaidyas tried their best, but nothing seemed to help the ailing king.

Now that he sensed his end was near, Gangadhar Rao became even more anxious about the fact that he might die without an heir. He had good reason to be.

The then governor-general, Lord Dalhousie, had formulated the much-hated Doctrine of Lapse.

According to this law, if an Indian ruler passed away without a natural son, the British would use that as a reason to annex the kingdom. This had already happened in the states of Satara and Nagpur. To prevent this, Gangadhar Rao was eager to adopt a child now. It so happened that some of his Newalkar relatives were visiting him for the Dussehra celebrations. Among them was Vasudev Rao, who had a five-year-old son named Ananda. The king decided to adopt this child and Vasudev agreed. 20 November was chosen as the date for the ceremony.

## Lord Dalhousie's infamous Doctrine of Lapse

The Doctrine of Lapse was an annexation policy widely applied by Lord Dalhousie, who was the governor-general of India between 1848 and 1856. According to the doctrine, any princely state or territory under the direct influence of the East India Company, as a vassal state under the British Subsidiary System, would automatically be annexed if the ruler was either 'manifestly incompetent or died without a direct heir'.

In his own words: 'I hold that on all occasions where heirs natural shall fail, the territory should be made to lapse, and adoption should not be permitted, excepting in those cases in which some strong political reason may render it expedient . . .' Using this excuse, Dalhousie brought many Indian states directly under British rule.

# 6 ✦ The Blow Falls

Anxious crowds had been gathering around the palace ever since news of the king's illness spread. Temple bells tolled through the city as his subjects prayed for his welfare. Gangadhar Rao's worries about the future of his kingdom and his wife added to his suffering. On 19 November he wrote a letter to Major Ellis, the political sub-agent of Jhansi. He informed him about his decision to adopt Ananda, and pleaded that he acknowledge the child as his heir and treat his queen kindly if he passed away. The Major was invited to attend the ceremony along with a Captain Martin. All the prominent citizens of Jhansi were present, too.

> *During the British rule, a political resident or political agent represented the government in Indian states. He maintained contact with rulers and looked after British interests. These agents played an important role in political affairs and often exerted great influence.*

The ritual was conducted at Gangadhar Rao's bedside. The boy's father gave up his claims and Ananda was proclaimed to be the son of Gangadhar Rao and

Lakshmibai. His name was changed to Damodar Rao, and his adoptive father gave him his blessings. All the others left after being offered gifts and the customary attar and paan, but the two British officers were asked to stay back, along with Moropant and the king's ministers. The queen was present, of course, but behind the purdah. Gangadhar Rao dictated a *kharita* or letter for Ellis's senior, D.A. Malcolm, the political agent for the region of Bundelkhand, Gwalior and Rewa. He gave it to Ellis, in which he again prayed that, 'In consideration of my loyalty, the government should treat the child with kindness. The administration of the state should be vested in my widow during her lifetime as the sovereign of this principality and mother of the child adopted.'

The letter was barely finished when a fit of convulsions suddenly overcame the king. Ellis and Martin left immediately. Gangadhar Rao's condition took a turn for the worse after the British officers departed. But after a while he felt a little better and immediately sent for Ellis again. Ellis arrived, along with a physician, Dr Allen.

'I just wanted to remind you that your government signed a treaty with Ramchandra Rao,' the raja said, his voice faltering. It was an effort for him to continue, but he went on. 'My father's descendants and family members were to be acknowledged as his successors to the throne of Jhansi. I beg you to honour this agreement.'

'Don't worry, Raja sa'ab,' Ellis said. 'Malcolm sa'ab instructed me to bring the medical officer here for your treatment, so I've brought Dr Allen. He is carrying some medicines that should help you. Can you tell him about your problem?'

Gangadhar described his symptoms in detail. The effort seemed to exhaust him.

'It appears to be an acute case of blood dysentery,' the doctor said. 'But I have something which should help. Raja sa'ab ... please take this.'

Gangadhar's eyes fluttered open. 'What is it?' he gazed blankly at the doctor at first. Then, 'No, no,' he said in a faint but firm voice. 'I cannot abandon my dharma ... take medicine ... from an untouchable foreigner.'

Moropant and the minister exchanged glances. 'Maybe if it is mixed with Gangajal . . .?' Moropant suggested. Gangadhar seemed to consider it for a while, then shook his head. Ellis pursed his lips, while the doctor shrugged helplessly. They lingered for a while and finally left. Later Ellis sent the medicine again with a Brahmin, but Gangadhar Rao refused it once more.

The day passed by slowly. An anxious night followed, as the king continued to slip in and out of consciousness. Morning came but did not offer much hope. All the mantras being chanted by priests and the donations of gold and cows did not seem to be of any help. Lakshmibai sat by her husband's bedside, sponging his face and offering him sips of water.

Around one in the afternoon he groaned in a faint voice, 'Gangajal ...'

A tremor shook the queen's frame. Moropant's face was grim as he looked at the prime minister. An attendant hurried up with a silver pot of sacred Ganga water, and

Lakshmibai poured it into his mouth with unsteady hands. Moments later the king stopped breathing.

A heart-rending cry burst from Lakshmbai's lips. She, who had never been known to break down, was beside herself with grief. Young Damodar clung to his mother and wept, too, unable to comprehend this sudden catastrophe. He was still dazed when he performed his father's last rites on the banks of Lake Lakshmi Tal that lay near the Mahalakshmi temple. The whole of Jhansi was sunk in grief. Ellis, who had joined the funeral procession, stood and watched the cremation along with another British officer.

### The Major and the Rani

Major Ellis was considered sympathetic to Lakshmibai, and it is reported that it went against him in his career. In *Rani,* a novel by Jaishree Misra, the author has shown that he was in love with her. This led to many protests and the chief minister, Mayawati, banned the book in Uttar Pradesh in February 2008.

# 7 ✳ Hard Times

Major Ellis immediately forwarded the news of Gangadhar's death to Kaitha, where the senior political agent Malcolm was based. Malcolm further sent this information to the governor-general, Lord Dalhousie, without any delay on 25 November, along with the kharita the Maharaja had entrusted to Ellis. In his accompanying letter, he mentioned that the ruler of Jhansi had no right to adopt an heir without the Company's permission. Also, that the queen might be able and popular, but the Company's rule would be more beneficial for the people. He suggested that Lakshmibai be granted a pension of Rs 5,000 a month, and be allowed to retain all the personal property of the deceased king, along with the city palace of Jhansi.

After dispatching the letter, he instructed Ellis to muster the troops and make preparations to take charge. It so happened that Lord Dalhousie was on tour and did not respond to Malcolm's letter for around five months. In the meantime, oblivious to all this, Lakshmibai and her advisers were getting ready to proclaim Damodar Rao as the new ruler.

Gangadhar Rao's untimely death had shattered the Rani. However, her strong spirit could not be quelled that easily. She was deeply conscious of her responsibilities, towards her son as well as the citizens of Jhansi. As custom decreed, she donned the widow's white garments, removed her jewellery, but did not shave her head. In a move that surprised many, she came out of purdah and only maintained it when she had to meet the British.

Nana Sahib and his brothers arrived to share her grief, accompanied by Tantya Tope. Nana had his own share of problems. When Bajirao II died, the British had arbitrarily stopped the pension of Rs 8 lakh a year that was granted to the Peshwa and his descendants under a treaty. Nana sent a petition to the governor-general, even dispatched an envoy named Azimullah Khan to England to plead his case with Queen Victoria, but to no avail. Consequently, he was seething with discontent.

The fact that the British had increased their forces and added to their armoury had not gone unnoticed. But Lakshmibai continued her business of governance, assisted by her ministers. She held a daily durbar and attended to the grievances of her subjects. Perhaps she wished to demonstrate that she was perfectly capable of ruling the kingdom till her son came of age.

When a whole month passed without any reply from the governor-general, both Ellis and Malcolm became perturbed. And then, another claimant to the throne of Jhansi appeared—Sadashiv Rao Newalkar. He produced a family tree to prove that he was a direct descendant of the original Newalkar ruler, refuting the Rani's claim. Ellis was not prepared to entertain him. His sympathies lay with the queen. He even wrote to Malcolm in a letter dated 24 December 1853: 'I believe it would be unjust to reject Jhansi's right of adoption.' He cited the precedent of the neighbouring state of Orchha, where the king's adopted son had been recognized as his heir, as justification.

Malcolm, on the other hand, recommended Sadashiv's case in a letter dated 31 December 1853. Confident that he would carry the day, Sadashiv began to project himself as the next ruler of Jhansi. Lakshmibai remained unfazed. She felt it would be more prudent to wait for the governor-general's response. She had written a letter to him in December, enclosing the Newalkar family tree to show that Damodar was closely related to Gangadhar Rao.

Meanwhile, she continued to maintain a strict discipline in her routine: she would rise at four, then bathe and worship Lord Mahadev till eight o'clock. The court singers would sing bhajans while she prayed. After that she exercised, that is, practised horse riding, sword fencing, wrestling and archery. As mentioned earlier, she trained all her companions as well as several women from the city in these arts. They became famous later as her so-called Durga Dal. At eleven, she would feed the poor, then have her own meal.

After eating, she would rest for a while. Then at three in the afternoon, she would feed fishes with pellets of dough filled with slips of paper which had Rama written on them. These could be as many as 1,100 in number. This was her hour of contemplation, and she would not speak with anyone while doing this. It was followed with more exercise. In the evening she would listen to religious discourses and bhajans again. Then she would entertain visitors, perform her evening worship and have dinner. She was very particular about time, and followed this routine rigorously.

When several months passed without any news from Dalhousie, in February 1854, Lakshmibai sent another kharita, reiterating the same appeal. The Rani recalled the treaties of 1804, 1817 and 1842, and pointed out that in 1817 the rights of any heirs, whether natural or adopted, had been guaranteed.

But how could Dalhousie let go of this opportunity to apply his favourite Doctrine of Lapse? On 27 February 1854, he passed an order quoting the original treaty Shivrao Bhau had made in 1804. He had acknowledged that Jhansi was part of the Peshwa's territory—not an independent state. The Company was at liberty to do what it wished in such cases—concede the claim of an adopted heir or dismiss it out of hand. It had not accepted the adopted heir of the former ruler Ramchandra Rao. Consequently, in the interests of its citizens, Jhansi would now come under Company rule. The queen would receive whatever pension the political agent recommended.

Dalhousie and his three assistants Dorin, Lowe and Halliday signed this order and sent it to Malcolm with instructions. Malcolm forwarded it with great secrecy to Ellis, who received it on 15 March 1854.

Ellis did not waste any time communicating the news to the queen, and headed for the palace the very next day. Lakshmibai had already heard that he had received a reply and was waiting anxiously for the decision. The mood was, in general, hopeful because the queen and her advisers felt that their case had merit. Besides, Jhansi had always supported the British.

Moropant and the ministers received Ellis in the diwan-e-khas, or the reception room, meant for special guests. Little Damodar Rao sat there, too, along with the elders. The Rani sat behind a screen. She was dressed in a white chanderi sari, with a string of pearls around her neck, and diamond bangles on her wrists. Ellis greeted the queen and the others courteously. Then without any further niceties, he read out Dalhousie's order and Malcolm's directives in a clear loud voice. He announced that Jhansi was now under British rule. Major Ellis had been appointed administrator, and he would collect all the taxes from the general public.

The news fell on the assembled group like a sudden bolt of lightning. For a moment there was silence; then exclamations of dismay buzzed throughout the hall.

Suddenly a sweet but high-pitched voice rang out, slicing through the clamour. '*Main apni Jhansi nahi doongi!*' It was the queen.

Ellis blinked, then gazed with astonishment at the screen behind which the queen sat. But he recovered fast and replied, 'I am only communicating the orders of my superiors. You are not being treated unjustly and will receive a pension of Rs 5,000 a month along with other benefits. I tried my best, Rani Sahiba, but you have to accept the governor-general's decision.'

Lakshmibai cut him short. 'I do not want your pension,' she said firmly.

Ellis made no reply. He simply bowed and left, asking the prime minister to accompany him. He requested him to hand over the keys of the offices and the treasury immediately, which the elderly man did mechanically. Like everyone else, he was too stupefied to put up any resistance.

### Whose assets?

The British authorities were quite arbitrary when it came to ruling who should receive the assets of former rulers, and often appropriated them. Among many others, Dalip Singh, the son of Maharaja Ranjit Singh of Punjab, was deprived of his inheritance. In the end Damodar Rao, too, did not receive his adopted father's *khasgi daulati* or personal wealth, and had to survive on a meagre pension.

# 8 🗡 Weathering the Storm

In no time at all, the news swept through the city like an evil wind, casting a pall of gloom. And when the citizens of Jhansi heard the menacing sound of drums and the voice of the crier announcing that they were no longer subjects of their queen but of the British, all hope that it might be just a rumour vanished. The outlying territories were informed in a similar manner.

Life seemed to have turned upside down in Jhansi. Many people wept in despair and out of sympathy for their Rani, while others vented their fury in talks of resistance. Some timeservers prepared to switch sides. The army would have revolted if the queen had not commanded them to show restraint. In any case, the British were well prepared for such an eventuality.

Lakshmibai's reaction to Ellis's pronouncement had been spontaneous. Later, however, she made up her mind to face the inevitable. And she did it with good grace, though in her heart of hearts she had not given up the fight.

She cheered up her woebegone staff and asked them to bear this misfortune bravely. They would have to give up the fort to the British, so she asked them to begin preparations for her departure.

\* \* \*

There was much to be done. Although somewhere Lakshmibai still hoped to return, she did not wish to leave too much of what had belonged to Jhansi for the interlopers—particularly that which could provide them with military advantage. Three cannons were buried in the courtyard of the palace—one of them was the famous Karakbijli. A large tunnel led from the fort to the city palace, via the elephant's stable. The queen decided to have the entrance walled up. Then she had her personal belongings packed, and departed for the city palace.

The royal army had not faced any battles for a long time, though they would be drilled regularly. The British disbanded them with six months' salary. They had to surrender their uniforms and weapons, too. But the soldiers did not wish to leave without paying their respects to the Rani. She accepted their farewells, seated behind a screen, as one by one they offered their salaams with tears in their eyes.

The rest of the queen's employees were left unemployed, too, but without any severance pay. Some of them managed to get absorbed in the new government, but most of the jagirdars and small landowners lost their property and status. Many were compelled to take up jobs as petty officials.

It was not easy to come to terms with this catastrophe, neither for the queen nor the citizens. She continued to send letters protesting against the order, and dispatched her attorney Kashmiri Mull to Calcutta to explain her case properly. When these petitions had no effect, some of the prominent men of the city advised Lakshmibai to send a kharita to the Court of Directors in England, appealing against Dalhousie's decision. A leading English lawyer, John Lang, was visiting India and the queen decided to consult him. He, too, felt that this might help. Kashmiri Mull went, accompanied by an Englishman, to plead the queen's case. Lakshmibai spent Rs 60,000 on this trip. But like Azimullah before him, Kashmiri Mull, too, was unable to accomplish anything.

Malcolm finally wrote to Dalhousie, suggesting that the queen's dependants receive some support. A request was also made that Gangadhar Rao's personal assets or khasgi daulati be handed over to his wife. But now Dalhousie entered into legalities of a different kind. He proclaimed that while Damodar Rao had no political standing as Gangadhar Rao's heir, the government would acknowledge his civil rights to his adopted father's property. The raja's houses in Parola, Pune and Varanasi, along with the cash and jewellery that was left, would not be handed over to the queen, but held in trust for the minor heir by the Company's administrators. In this way the queen was deprived of even her husband's possessions.

The administration of the region was reorganized. Jhansi came under the control of Major Erskine, the divisional commissioner of Jabalpur, Sagar and Narmada. He was answerable to John Russel Colvin, the Lieutenant Governor of the North-Western Province. Both Malcolm and Ellis, who knew the Rani well, took up duties elsewhere. Captain Skene became commissioner of Jhansi in Ellis's place.

John Lang had suggested that the Rani provisionally accept the pension, but she refused. She even proclaimed that she would leave Jhansi and settle in Varanasi. This disturbed the British officials, because they knew it would create unrest in the city. Colvin appealed to Sir Robert Hamilton, who was the political agent of the governor-general for central India and had much better rapport with Indian rulers. Hamilton was finally able to persuade her to draw the pension.

It was a time of severe trial for Lakshmibai. Not only had she lost her husband, but was also dispossessed of almost all that had been an integral part of her existence after she married Gangadhar Rao—her status, her home and a major portion of her income. She was not even permitted to go on pilgrimage and shave her head at Varanasi, as was required of a widow. (Apparently, later she did *prayashchitta* or penance for this lapse.) Yet something very precious remained with her— the love and respect of the people of Jhansi. Equally important, she did not allow these painful experiences to cast her down.

She continued with her routine. She would rise early as before, perform her worship, then go riding for about three hours. After that she supervised Damodar's lessons with a tutor. She was deeply conscious that a proper education and disciplined habits would stand him in good stead throughout his life. Morning and evening, Damodar studied Persian with a maulvi and Sanskrit with a pandit. He participated enthusiastically in religious rituals along with his mother, and would help feed the fish with the pellets stuffed with the name of Rama.

It is said that he was very fond of sweets and did not want to eat anything else. Lakshmibai, who believed so strongly in physical fitness, took this matter in hand. 'Ananda,' she asked, using the name given to him by his parents, 'don't you wish to ride Siddhabaksh when you grow up? And go galloping around the city?'

'Of course,' Damodar replied. 'I want to lead the parade through the streets of Jhansi on Siddhabaksh. And ride as fast as you do!'

'But how will you manage to if you don't eat your vegetables and dal and chapattis?' she continued affectionately. 'You'll never grow tall and strong enough to climb Siddhabaksh. And why are you picking out all the nuts from that laddoo?'

Damodar wrinkled his nose. 'I don't like them!'

'Don't be so fussy, child,' his mother stroked his head. 'You must learn to eat everything, even if you don't like it.' Her eyes misted over, wondering what the future might hold for this boy who had been so cruelly deprived of his rights.

Little did she know that many more unpleasant experiences remained in store for her, too. The British were determined to drive home the point that they held the reins of the government now, and as a dethroned queen she would have to quietly accept each new humiliation. This was adding insult to injury.

## The riddle of the Rani

The Rani remained a figure of mystery to the British, because she remained behind the purdah when meeting officials. John Lang's description of her (mentioned in chapter 4) when he caught a brief glimpse of her, while young Damodar moved the curtain, has been quoted extensively.

Gangadhar Rao had paid off most of the enormous debt incurred by his elder brother Ramchandra Rao, but a sum of Rs 36,000 still remained. Colvin now decided to extract this amount from the Rani. He ordered that it be recovered in instalments from her meagre monthly pension of Rs 5,000. Lakshmibai was furious. Her pension barely covered her expenses, and as she said rightly, she could not be held liable for a debt incurred by the state of Jhansi. But Colvin would not entertain this line of reasoning. As was typical of most British officials, he was only concerned with adding to the treasury, and ordinary human concerns did not bother him at all.

Worse was to come. The Mahalakshmi temple was sacrosanct for Lakshmibai and the people of Jhansi, and the revenue of two villages was allotted for its maintenance. Gordon and Skene decided to confiscate those villages. Their justification was that the money was being squandered on the worship of idols, which was a total waste of resources. The queen objected, but Skene replied arrogantly, 'Your God is our responsibility.'

The temple could not function the way it had any more. The priests asked her to protest again, but Lakshmibai refused. If even the gods had been taken over by the foreign rulers, what could she do? Other temples suffered the same fate.

Skene and the Deputy Commissioner Gordon now introduced a new system of law and justice. Instead of the queen's durbar, people had to appeal to the administration for any kind of redress. A new profession sprang up—of lawyers and petition writers, though at that time no law examination existed. The Deputy Commissioner appointed advocates, the same way he handed out jobs in the government or zamindaris to people who flattered the officials of the new dispensation sufficiently.

Barely had the people of Jhansi come to terms with the takeover of the revenue of the Mahalakshmi and other temples, when their religious sentiments received another blow from their callous rulers. Only about eighty Englishmen lived in the city, but it was considered necessary to construct a slaughterhouse to cater to their eating habits. It was set up right in the middle of the city, and both cows and pigs were slaughtered there and the meat and skins were transported uncovered through the streets. This was offensive to both Hindus and Muslims. The queen remonstrated, but her objections were dismissed out of hand. As a subject people, the Indians were permitted no rights to even protest.

Little did the British know that all these acts were slowly adding to the deep resentment building up against them. They led a comfortable life within the spacious compounds of their bungalows, cut off from the general populace. And they were so confident of their dominant position that it did not strike them that the very people they had subdued with such ease might dare to contemplate any action against them.

After all, they were leading the country towards progress. An efficient police force maintained law and order, and schools were being opened to provide modern education. A network of roads and railways spread over the country, making travel far more convenient than it had ever been, while government jobs provided secure incomes. What else could anyone want?

Lakshmibai fell into the routine of her new existence. She continued to hone her riding skills and train women in the use of arms. Apart from Mandar, Sundar and Kashibai, other women of the city and nearby villages joined her as she exercised in the garden that lay below the slope behind the government library. Among them was Jhalkari Bai, a striking young woman who belonged to the Kori community.

> *As a young girl, Jhalkari had proved her bravery by killing a tiger with her axe while she was gathering firewood. She thus seemed a natural for the women's army Lakshmibai was training, sometimes described as the Durga Dal. Jhalkari was married to Pooran Kori, who showed his mettle in defending Jhansi later. She bore a striking resemblance to the Rani.*

The library, a treasure house of rare manuscripts collected by her late husband, stood in front of the city palace where she lived and was thankfully still in her control. But now another issue cropped up which added to the unbearable list of her grievances. Damodar turned seven in 1855, and according to custom his sacred thread ceremony had to be performed at this age. If Gangadhar Rao had been alive, there would have been a grand celebration.

Whatever her circumstances, Lakshmibai was determined to mark it with suitable festivities. Even if she kept it as simple as possible, she had many obligations to fulfil and the ritual would not cost less than one lakh. Gifts would be distributed to dependents and relatives, a proper feast had to be given and the actual ceremony itself had its own requirements. But from where would the money come?

The British had held back Rs 6 lakh from Gangadhar Rao's estate, claiming they were keeping it in trust for Damodar. They had also confiscated some gold and jewellery. The queen decided to ask for 1 lakh from these funds. To justify her request, she prepared a list of expenses with the help of her father Moropant.

Colvin's reply cast a severe dampener on her enthusiasm. He said that the amount was too much to spend on a religious ceremony, and Damodar might dispute the expenditure when he was old enough to claim his inheritance.

The Rani's cup of bitterness brimmed over. When they heard the news, some of the leading businessmen of the city came forward to offer financial help. But her contention was—why should she incur obligations when

Damodar already possessed sufficient funds? After much discussion it was decided that they offer guarantees to the British against the sum that would be released. The queen conveyed the information to Colvin, saying that five people—Moropant, Jaipurwala, Lakshmichand and two others—had furnished a bond agreeing to pay 20,000 sikkas each in the Jhansi currency in case Damodar raised any objections. Colvin accepted this, and the money was dispersed.

Damodar's thread ceremony was observed in a style appropriate to his position. All the customary rituals were performed, and a grand feast and musical recitals followed. It is said that old friends like Nana Sahib, his brothers and Tantya Tope attended it along with local jagirdars and the leading citizens of Jhansi. But the shabby treatment meted out to her still rankled and Lakshmibai abandoned all hope that she would ever receive justice from the British.

**What was the last straw?**
British writers like T.R. Holmes, who wrote the *History of the Indian Mutiny*, Sir John William Kaye and Col. G.B. Malleson, the authors of *A History of the Indian Mutiny of 1857–58*, all agree on one point—Colvin's unjust demand that Lakshmibai pay her husband's debts from her small pension was a very important factor in turning her against the British. These writers are not generally sympathetic to the Rani otherwise.

# 10 ✳ Grievances Multiply

The Rani of Jhansi was not the only one who had grievances against the British. Discontent had been simmering throughout the country for quite some time. It was not only the dethroned rulers who had a reason to complain; the common people were being ground under British boots, too, as their armies continued a relentless march, occupying more and more land.

The East India Company had entered the country in the guise of traders, but they had now become its rulers. They had employed a mixture of force and cunning to advance their interests. As the Union Jack began to flutter over larger swathes of Indian territory, the condition of the general public deteriorated. Soon it became far worse than it had ever been under the local rajas; not that all the kings had selflessly attended to the welfare of their own people. But there had always been a sense of identification which was totally missing in the foreign rulers, whose main purpose was to exploit their acquisitions to the fullest.

There was an initial resistance, and small rebellions did flare up. However, they were squashed with incredible harshness. An Englishman could get away with the most violent crime against an Indian, and the latter never hope to receive redress. Whether a galloping horse ridden by an Englishman trampled a small child, or a carriage ran over an old man, the guilty party could get away with impunity if he were white. If the victim dared to protest, he was more likely to be beaten viciously or thrown into jail.

The allure of a well-paid job with the foreign government turned out to be a bitter illusion for many. There was no respect for Indian religions, no understanding of local culture and no empathy towards local customs. Many who joined the army in order to earn a living found, to their dismay, that the orders they received often violated their religious code of conduct. Refusal meant severe punishment, even death. In addition, the salary an Indian received was far below that given to a white man.

The new revenue laws were a torment for farmers. If their crops failed for reasons beyond their control, they could not hope for any leniency. The new breed of zamindars instituted by the British was as cruel as its masters. A vast body of retainers employed by former kings, who were thrown out of jobs when their employers lost their kingdoms, swelled the number of the disaffected. As if it were not enough, missionaries roamed the country urging people to abandon their faith and adopt that of the conqueror.

The unjust annexation of Awadh was another provocation. The people began to feel that their very identity as Indians was being endangered. Soon the country was in a state of ferment. Posters appeared in Delhi and other places, asking people to prepare to fight the foreign invader. In a mysterious development, chapattis and lotus flowers began to be sent from village to village. They were said to be signs informing the public to prepare for the approaching insurrection. On market days, sadhus, fakirs and dervishes foretold the end. It was prophesied that the British rule would only last for a hundred years—from the fateful Battle of Plassey in 1757 to 1857, a year that was fast approaching.

There were scores of grievances against the British, but the introduction of the Enfield Pritchett 53 rifle provided the spark that triggered off the rebellion in 1857. The cartridges used in this rifle were smeared with fat and wrapped in greased paper. The soldiers had to bite off the rear end before putting the cartridge into the barrel. The fat used was extracted from cows and pigs, and thus abhorrent to both Hindus and Muslims.

At this time an incident occurred in the army cantonment of Dumdum, near Kolkata, which caused further aggravation. In January 1857, a low caste sepoy asked a Brahmin for his water pot, so he could quench his thirst. The Brahmin objected, saying he would lose caste if he let him use it. The other laughed and said, 'What's the point of making such a fuss? You're going to lose caste anyway, when you put the cartridges smeared with animal fat into your mouth.'

The sepoy went and told his comrades at once, who became very agitated. After discussing the issue for a while, they decided to ask their commanding officers for clarification. The officers assured them that their feelings would be taken into consideration. When the matter was reported to General Hearsey, he informed Lord Canning, the new governor-general. Canning suggested that some other oil be used for greasing the cartridges, and different commanding officers were consulted on the best way to deal with this problem.

But the soldiers did not have much faith in the British promises. They lost no time in dispatching letters to other cantonments, warning their compatriots throughout the country. In an amazingly short while, thousands of such letters reached sepoys in different regions.

Matters were now reaching explosion point. On 26 February 1857, the 19th Native Infantry Regiment stationed in Behrampur, Bengal, was asked to test the new rifles. The soldiers refused. Colonel Mitchell, the commanding officer, tried to persuade them but without success. The very next day the regiment rebelled. They were ordered to return to their barracks and dismissed from service on 31 March.

It was a lone sepoy, however, who actually lit the fuse that set off the conflagration. This happened on the afternoon of 29 March—a Sunday. The sepoys of the 34th regiment, posted in Barrackpur, heard one of their comrades calling out to them. His name was Mangal Pandey, and he was pacing the regimental ground with his musket in hand, shouting, 'Come out, everyone! Get ready to fight the firangis if you wish to save your castes.'

The matter was reported to the adjutant Lt Baugh, who hurried to the scene. Pandey took a shot at him, and then fired at Sergeant-Major Hewson, who came to his rescue. Hewson ordered an Indian junior officer, Jemadar Ishwari Prasad, to come to his help, but he would not obey the order. Eventually, when General John Hearsey appeared on the scene, Mangal Pandey was overpowered and put in prison. He was condemned to death along with Ishwari Prasad. The two were executed in April and the regiment disbanded.

Most of the soldiers belonged to the provinces of Awadh and Bihar. The annexation of Awadh had already deprived many of them of their rights as landowners. They returned to their homes burning with resentment against their British employers.

### 1857 in films

The 1857 War of Independence has been the subject of many films. In recent times, the popular film *Mangal Pandey: The Rising* starring Aamir Khan and Rani Mukherji, directed by Ketan Mehta, was released in 2005.

The award-winning 1977 film *Junoon*, based on Ruskin Bond's novella *The Flight of Pigeons*, was set in Lucknow during the mutiny. It was directed by Shyam Benegal and starred Shashi Kapoor, Shabana Azmi, Jennifer Kendall, Naseeruddin Shah and Nafisa Ali.

Satyajit Ray's 1978 film *Shatranj ke Khiladi*, based on Munshi Premchand's short story of the same name, was set in 1856, during the time when Awadh was annexed. It starred Amjad Khan as Nawab Wajid Ali Shah, Shabana Azmi, Sanjeev Kumar, Saeed Jaffrey and Richard Attenborough, with Amitabh Bachchan's voiceover.

# 11 ✱ The Rebellion

The first serious uprising actually occurred in Meerut, which was a large cantonment. The unsympathetic commander of the 3rd Bengal Light Cavalry insisted that ninety soldiers drill with the new rifles on 24 April. When eighty-five of them refused, he court-martialled them and put them in shackles on 9 May. The next day the remaining soldiers rebelled and set their companions and other prisoners free. Then they marched to Delhi to ask the Mughal emperor Bahadur Shah Zafar to assume power. They overpowered the British troops stationed there and occupied the Red Fort. Bahadur Shah Zafar was proclaimed emperor of Hindustan and a twenty-one-gun salute fired.

This rebellion soon spread all over northern India.

\* \* \*

When Lakshmibai had been forced to leave the fort and her troops dismissed, the 12th Native Infantry of the Bengal Army occupied it. Captain Alexander Skene was appointed the political superintendent, while Captain Dunlop held the post of commanding officer of the garrison.

The sepoys stationed at Jhansi, most of whom were from Awadh, had been regularly receiving news of the rebellion flaring up in other parts of the country. Each new incident, filtering through to them, intensified their patriotic sentiments and hatred for the foreign rulers. The British officers were conscious that the situation was inflammatory, but they believed that the men in Jhansi were under their control.

Skene wrote to his superior: 'I am going on the principle of showing perfect confidence and I am quite sure I am right.' All the same, they took precautions. The cantonment area was situated at a distance of two miles from the Jhansi Fort, which lay to the south of the city. The officers' quarters, the jail and the Star Fort, a small star-shaped building in which all the arms, ammunition and provisions were stored, were located in the cantonment. Dunlop had the women and children sent to the Jhansi Fort. The officers did not want to make their apprehensions obvious, so they continued to attend to their daily duties in the cantonment and slept in the fort.

Skene and the others were taken by surprise when the sepoys, led by Havaldar Jauna Gurbaksh Singh, struck on 4 June. They occupied the Star Fort, along with its ammunition and provisions, without any difficulty. Dunlop immediately informed Colonel Kirk at Naogaon and requested help from Gwalior and Sagar. By evening all the British officers, civil and military, had moved into the fort. When Lakshmibai heard what had happened, she sent Dewan Lakshman Rao Bande to Skene with the advice that the British leave for Sagar or Datia right away. She had initially offered to keep the women and children with her in the palace, against the advice of those close to her, but Skene felt they were better off in the Jhansi Fort.

The British requested her for support, but Lakshmibai well knew that it would be impossible to protect the sixty-five British nationals—men, women and children—sheltering in the Jhansi Fort, along with their staff and some Indian Christians. She only had a personal guard of forty men, while the rebels were 600 in number. She informed Skene that her resources were unequal to the situation, but he did not take her seriously.

For two days there was no further trouble. But on 6 June, Dunlop and another officer, Taylor, decided to address their troops. They were quite confident that they would be able to bring them back under their command and harshly ordered the sepoys to return to their duties. The consequences were disastrous. Led by Risaldar Kale Khan, the soldiers shot them dead. When the news spread through the city, those inside the fort quickly shut the gates and barricaded themselves. A few Englishmen were left outside and the sepoys soon picked them off and surrounded the fort. All this time, at great personal risk, the Rani had been sending food for the people sheltering in the fort. Now, however, the British began to panic and out of distrust killed some of their Indian servants who had accompanied them there when they fled the rebellious sepoys. Three British men headed for the palace in disguise, intending to ask the queen for help. They never got there. One of them, Andrews, was killed by the son of a man named Jharhukumar, whom he had insulted for no reason earlier.

Conditions began to deteriorate inside the fort and soon there was nothing left to eat. When she heard, it is said, Lakshmibai had a large number of rotis cooked and sent her trusted companions Mandar, Sundar and Kashibai to deliver them. To prevent the sepoys from finding out, they used a secret tunnel. The besieged British accepted the food gratefully. Apparently, Colonel Martin noticed the tunnel and used it to escape when things went out of hand. Later, he vouched that the queen had actually helped the beleaguered English, but the investigating officials preferred to believe other accounts.

Martin felt so strongly about this that later he wrote to Damodar Rao, clearing Lakshmibai's name.

Colonel Martin's letter to Damodar Rao:
*20-8-1889*

*We have treated your unfortunate mother with extreme injustice and cruelty. Nobody knows the truth as much as I do. The innocent woman of a noble character was not in the least involved with the massacre of June 1857. Furthermore, she supplied food for two consecutive days to the English under siege inside the fort. She brought in a hundred armed soldiers from Karhera to help the English, but they were sent back on request of Captain Skene. She had repeatedly requested Captain Skene and Gordon to flee to the king of Datia for safe shelter.*

The officers inside had been attempting to protect the fort. A skilled archer among the sepoys, however, shot down Gordon, who was in command. This threw the defence into disarray and on 8 June, Skene decided to surrender on the condition that they would be allowed to proceed to Sagar unharmed. Hakim Saleh Ahmed, an elderly physician, conducted the negotiations. When they were reassured of their safety, the party left the fort and were taken to a place called Jhokan Bagh. Then all hell broke loose. A large group of soldiers suddenly appeared and shouted out that the British did not deserve to be spared. Bakshish Ali, the jail warden, who had been humiliated by Skene earlier, led the massacre. He claimed to be acting on Risaldar Kale Khan's orders. All the men, women and children, including Skene, were cut down mercilessly.

The bloodbath horrified the common people. But charged with the excitement of what they considered a victory, the disorderly sepoys made for the queen's palace. Kale Khan shouted out the slogan:

God rules this land,
The emperor rules the country,
This kingdom belongs to the queen!

Lakshmibai was stunned at this turn of events. But she had to maintain her composure and try to salvage the situation, highly inflammable as it was. She came to her window to face this mass of restless, bloodthirsty men. 'We have rid you of the firangis!' the soldiers yelled. 'We're going to Delhi! Give us money for our expenses! At least three lakh of rupees!'

'I would give it to you, but I have no money. You know the British took everything,' Lakshmibai replied firmly.

'We will loot the city then!' voices rang out.

The queen felt really apprehensive now. She knew what would happen if they went on the rampage.

She was relieved when the Risaldar said, 'Bai Sahiba, the men are hungry. We just want to leave for Delhi immediately and join the other freedom fighters. Please help us!'

Lakshmibai was in a quandary. She was shocked by the massacre and did not wish to support the perpetrators. However, her duty was to keep the citizens of Jhansi safe. So she took off the valuable diamond necklace she was wearing. 'This is worth at least one lakh,' she said. 'Take it, I have nothing else left.' The Risaldar grabbed it and the soldiers marched off, repeating the slogan.

The Rani was intelligent enough to realize that a volatile situation was brewing. Weighed down with anxiety, she first sent instructions that the dead British be given a decent burial. Then she sent a letter to the commissioner of Jabalpur, Major Erskine, on 12 June, informing him about the turn of events.

Lakshmibai knew Jhansi was in a more vulnerable position than ever, now that the British presence had gone. It was open to attack from all sides, and she had no army worth the name to protect it. It was a ready-made opportunity not only for ambitious neighbours but pretenders to the throne as well. Only a very strong arm could keep matters under control.

The two messengers she had sent to Erskine had been disguised as beggars, carrying her letters in a hollow stick because there was a real possibility that they might be attacked on the way. Fortunately they managed to reach him with her letter, though it is said they were held up on the way and asked to part with whatever little they possessed. The commissioner sent a reply, instructing her to govern Jhansi on behalf of the British till their troops arrived to take charge. He ordered all the officials to obey her.

Strangely, after giving her this charge, Erskine decided to proclaim her a 'rebel queen'. Despite all attempts to do the right thing, the British always managed to find fault with Lakshmibai. At Fort William, a warrant was prepared against her, blaming her for the killings and condemning her to be hanged. Even though the accounts of the few who escaped the massacre—an Englishman and a few Indian Christians—were contradictory and even inaccurate, she was painted as the villain of the piece. Even some historians, who should have known better, have insisted on making her party to the murders of innocent women and children.

## Guilty without trial

The British authorities blamed the Rani for being behind the massacre at Jhansi, without even listening to her side of the story. It is said she sent a letter to Colonel Fraser, the chief commissioner of the North-Western Provinces who was stationed at Agra, giving details of the actual events. However, he didn't even glance at it.

Prejudiced statements by people who had escaped and testified against her were taken as gospel truth, though they were riddled with discrepancies. She was condemned without a hearing, even by many historians.

# 12 ✳ The Rani Rules

When the queen took over the government of Jhansi, she proved to be more than a capable ruler. The first thing she did was to appoint ministers and raise an army from among those loyal to her. 3,240 soldiers had been dismissed when her army was disbanded. She recalled all of them. This force was made up of men belonging to all castes and creeds. Bundelas and Thakurs were recruited along with people of humble origins like the Kachchis, Koris and Telis. Afghans, locally described as vilayatis, and Pathans enlisted, too, and more than proved their loyalty later. The cannons that the British had disabled were unearthed, restored, and the fort manned properly.

The city had been teetering on the verge of anarchy. But now that there was a functioning administration, law and order was restituted. The outlying regions also received attention and the poorest farmers were spared from paying the previous years' taxes. Moreover, in order to provide employment, the Rani encouraged manufacture and set up a mint.

Lakshmibai had abandoned purdah after her husband's death and observed it only when she met the British. She was particular about her appearance and always dressed regally, mostly in male attire—a blue silk jacket, tight trousers and a turban. A sword would be tucked into the silk sash around her waist, which had a hilt and scabbard studded with rubies. Occasionally she would wear a white sari—being a widow—with a pearl necklace and diamond bangles.

While riding out, she usually dressed in a Pathan outfit and is said to have proclaimed that she had given up her widow's dharma to follow the dharma of the ruler. Adopting a male costume and one that was considered Muslim, despite her deeply religious nature, showed how flexible she was in responding to the need of the times. Along with the measures she took to improve the lot of her people, her charismatic personality inspired loyalty and drew many enthusiastic followers.

However, tough times came very soon. Sadashiv Rao Narayana, a great-grandson of Gangadhar Rao's ancestor Sadashiv Pant, had laid claim to the throne of Jhansi earlier. He still lived in Parola, the ancestral place of the Newalkars, and owned an estate there. When he heard that the British had been driven out of Jhansi, he thought it was a ready-made opportunity for him. He arrived with a force of 3,000 men and captured the fort of Karhera, which lay in the queen's territory. On 16 June, he crowned himself the king of Jhansi and began to plunder the surrounding countryside, demanding allegiance.

Lakshmibai took immediate action. She sent an army led by Jawahar Singh, one of the landowners of the neighbourhood, who was also one of her ministers. He routed Sadashiv Rao, who fled to Narwar in Gwalior. The queen sent a force in pursuit, and he was taken prisoner and lodged in the dungeons of the Jhansi Fort.

Barely had she dealt with this threat when another reared up—from the neighbouring states of Orchha and Datia. The Rajput rulers of the region had always resented the presence of a Maratha kingdom in their midst. Ladaiya Rani, who ruled Orchha since her son was a minor, seized the opportunity to team up with the state of Datia and attack Jhansi. Her minister Nathe Khan set out with a strong army of 25,000 soldiers to invade the kingdom on 10 August. But before he attacked, Nathe Khan sent a message to the queen saying that if she surrendered, she would receive the same pension and other benefits that the British had given her.

Lakshmibai rejected this offer scornfully, though her advisers told her she was in no position to fight back. She requested Jawahar Singh, Raghunath Singh Nauner, Dalip Singh and other leading landowners to support her. They immediately put together a force that was capable of taking on the enemy. Raja Mardan Singh of Banpur joined her, too, and contributed cannons and other military supplies.

Once again, the Rani wrote and informed the British of the situation, asking for help; technically, she was ruling Jhansi on their behalf. She got no response, however.

Soon news arrived that the enemy forces were moving towards Jhansi. Lakshmibai assembled her troops and came out in battle gear. After she had acknowledged their salute, she asked Jawahar Singh to come forward and tied an orange thread on his wrist. This indicated that she had appointed him the commander-in-chief of the army. Jawahar Singh placed his sword at her feet, as a gesture of loyalty. She picked it up and returned it to him. All the men cheered, drums were beaten and the war trumpets blown. The Jhansi soldiers were in fine fettle for battle now.

In the beginning, the larger army prevailed. Lakshmibai allowed Nathe Khan to advance towards the fortress without much opposition. When Khan's forces were close enough, the Jhansi gunners blasted them with cannon balls. Nathe Khan was targeting the six gates of the city, hoping to break in. The Rani spared no effort in supervising the defence. She was constantly on the move, encouraging her soldiers and keeping up their morale when the course of battle seemed to go against them. For twenty days, Nathe Khan's army kept up the assault. However, the Jhansi artillery won the day. Karakbijli, the famous cannon with a lion shaped mouth, had a long range and finally the enemy forces were compelled to flee. Ladaiya Rani had to concede defeat, and paid war damages to Jhansi.

Lakshmibai's charisma and her genuine concern for her men also had an effect on this outcome.

> *In the fight with Nathe Khan when the wounded men were brought into the city, the Bai herself would insist on being present when their wounds were being dressed. Her very presence soothed their pain, and they felt sufficiently rewarded by the kind and sympathetic interest*

The victory was celebrated with a grand parade.
The Rani distributed gifts, honours and awarded
pensions to the families of those who had fallen
in battle.

### An Indian Joan of Arc
The Rani's British foes described her as a 'Joan of Arc',
and like Joan of Arc she came to a violent end.

They were quite puzzled by her ability to lead armies
and create effective strategies for war. Many historians
have remarked on this, too. In the novel *Jhansi ki Rani*,
novelist Vrindavan Lal Verma has depicted her as
meticulously studying previously fought wars to hone
her skills, thus showing her military expertise was not a
fluke. The book is based on information gathered from
both written and oral sources.

# 13 ✦ The Coming of the Storm

Lakshmibai well knew that she was ruling on borrowed time. There was no telling when the British would return and once they did, she would receive the same unjust treatment that had always been her lot. Now, however, she was determined not to give in without a fight. For this reason she kept her army in readiness. She recruited more forces and drilled them regularly. She also kept in touch with Tantya Tope and Nana Sahib, and maintained her relationship with two of her important allies, Raja Mardan Singh of Banpur and Bakhtab Ali, the Raja of Shahgarh.

In the meantime, she continued to send letters to the British informing them of the precariousness of her position. They, on the other hand, were well aware of what was going on in Jhansi. Their spies kept them properly updated. They knew that new guns were being manufactured, old ones restored, ammunition and gunpowder being prepared.

Still, life seemed quite normal in Jhansi between September 1857 and February 1858, though fierce battles raged in most parts of northern India.

The Rani maintained the routine she followed earlier. After her morning exercises, her bath and puja, she would meet her 150 sardars and other officials. Those who did not attend would be asked to explain their absence. After lunch and a brief period of rest, she held court in an imposing manner. She would be seated on a throne with two attendants standing on each side holding gold and silver-plated maces. Her prime minister, Dewan Lakshman Rao Bande, would present the documents she needed to inspect, and she would go through them and pass orders. Sometimes she wrote them herself, but usually she dictated them to clerks.

The Rani had been an expert horsewoman since childhood and was also skilled at assessing horses. No one could palm off a second-rate steed on her. It is said that once her supplier of horses showed her a beautiful silver-grey mare and told her that he was unable to sell the horse. The moment the mare was mounted she would get restless and throw off the rider. Lakshmibai tried her out and was able to retain her seat. She bought the mare and told the dealer that the animal had some injury that caused pain when a rider's legs touched her side. Later it was discovered that a nail was stuck near her ribcage, which had probably come off a saddle. Lakshmibai had the nail extracted and this very mare later became famous as her beloved Sarangi.

The queen cared deeply for the welfare of the common people. Once, during the severe winter of 1857–58, she saw the poor huddled around fires, shivering in the cold. She immediately stepped down from her palanquin and asked them to come to the palace after four days. Then she summoned the tailors of the city and asked them to stitch woollen jackets and caps.

Hundreds of needy people received clothing and blankets to fight the bitter weather. Such was her magnanimity!

By 20 September 1857, the British had taken control of Delhi again. And by November, Lucknow was conquered. Nana Sahib was defeated in Kanpur in July by Havelock and had fled, but Tantya was keeping the campaign going along with Nana's nephew Rao Sahib.

Lakshmibai well knew that her turn would be coming soon. The British had already labelled her the 'Jezebel of India'. Moreover, all the signs were ominous. A new governor-general, Lord Canning, had taken over from Dalhousie. He considered the Rani of Jhansi such a serious threat that a highly experienced general, Sir Hugh Rose, was sent for. A diplomat by profession, Sir Hugh was also one of the best commanders in the British army, having proved his bravery in hand-to-hand battle, along with his capacity as a leader, in both the Turko-Egyptian and the Crimean War. At fifty-seven, he was far from young and had immense knowledge of military matters.

Hugh Rose led a well-trained army—the Central India Field Force. It consisted of troops that had been hurriedly dispatched from England, along with the best of the loyal Indian soldiers. They were supported by a contingent from Hyderabad: the Nizam, like Scindia of Gwalior and the ruler of Nepal, had provided a great deal of assistance to the British.

The campaign plans were, however, to be drawn up by Sir Robert Hamilton, the governor-general's political agent for central India, along with the supreme command in Calcutta. Though Jhansi did not lie under his jurisdiction, Hamilton had a great deal of experience in handling political affairs in central India and was familiar with the geography of the region. And he was somewhat sympathetic towards the Rani, who maintained correspondence with him and kept putting forth her point of view as long as it was possible.

On 6 January 1858, a formidable force of infantry, cavalry and artillery set out from the cantonment of Mhow, near Indore in central India, under the command of Sir Hugh Rose. Soon after they left, they had to veer from the original course that had been laid out for them and head towards Sagar, following an appeal by the officers of the British garrison stationed there, who feared danger from their own sepoys. A regiment of the 42nd Native Infantry had indeed risen against the British. But while they joined the army of Bakhtab Ali, the ruler of Shahgarh, they did not harm the English people who had taken shelter in Sagar fort. Many of the sepoys of the 31st regiment, also at Sagar, had risen too, though some remained loyal.

Bakhtab Ali, Raja Mardan Singh of Banpur and Mohammad Fazil Khan of Rahatgarh were all active in this region and had attacked the British at Sagar, Damoh and Jabalpur with their own armies along with the sepoys who had left different regiments posted in central India. The rebel leaders received news about the new development and decided to try and beat Hugh Rose on the way itself. The first engagement took place on 26 January at the Rahatgarh fort, which lay 48 km south-west of Sagar. This fort occupied a vantage point on the route to Sagar and held out a formidable challenge. Rose shelled it with his heavy siege artillery all through 27 January. Led by Mohammad Fazil Khan, an army consisting mostly of the local peasantry, along with a few sepoys, put up a determined defence from within the fort. On 28 January, the doughty fighter Raja Mardan Singh appeared and harassed the enemy from the rear. But Rose kept up his attack unabated, and in spite of all their efforts the citadel finally fell to the British. The next battle at Barodia, too, went against the Indians, despite Raja Mardan Singh's inspired leadership.

After these two encounters, Sagar posed no problem at all. There was no military action there and Rose arrived there on 2 February and halted to replenish his supplies. The 'siege train'—a cavalcade of carts and pack animals that had come from Bombay to provide support to his army—was restocked. Enormous guns, so heavy that only elephants could drag them, formed part of his artillery, along with howitzers and mortars. Rose needed more elephants for these guns and was able to requisition them in Sagar. Also, the soldiers who had come from England were dressed in thick red and blue uniforms, which were not suitable for battle. These were replaced with stone coloured cotton ones, better suited to the Indian summer and also less visible to sharpshooters.

Rose's army began its onward journey on 27 February. Sagar lay at a distance of merely 193 km from Jhansi. But the rebels occupied the country in between. The terrain was extremely rugged, with rows of hills, dense forests and deep gorges, making passage difficult. Three passes had to be crossed as well—Narut, Madanpur and Dhamoni. Raja Mardan Singh defended Narut, erecting a barricade of rocks and boulders, while the Raja of Shahgarh manned Madanpur with his Bundela soldiers. Hugh Rose decided to target the easier Madanpur pass, and sent only a small force to keep Mardan Singh busy at Narut.

This turned out to be the most challenging battle so far for Rose. Two ranges of densely forested hills flanked the pass, which was a narrow ravine. The defending forces had placed cannons not only inside the gorge but on both sides, too. Their men lay in ambush in the jungles, waiting to attack the enemy. As the British began to climb up the pass, the Raja's gunfire exploded in full force. Rose's artillery was far superior, but the Raja's relentless assault took such a toll that he had to order his soldiers to retreat. The men were falling rapidly and had to take shelter behind their guns. Even the general's horse was shot from under him and he barely escaped with his life. However, this did not last long. The British advantage of better equipment prevailed, and eventually the Indian troops had to fall back.

The rebels had underestimated the strength of the British armoury and this defeat came as a serious blow to the cause. All the same, they did not give up and continued to harass Rose's army till it reached Jhansi. He had to take the forts of Serai, Maraura and finally Chanderi before arriving in the vicinity of Jhansi on 20 March.

## What happened to Nana Sahib?

The British recaptured Kanpur, Nana Sahib's stronghold, in July 1857. While Tantya and Rao Sahib continued to fight on elsewhere, Nana Sahib vanished. He was never found, and there were rumours that he had died of malaria or escaped to Nepal with his wives. There was even a story of his being spotted in Constantinople (Istanbul). Strangely, several people turned themselves in to the British, claiming to be Nana. Famous author Jules Verne even wrote a novel titled *The End of Nana Sahib*. But Nana's real end remains one of history's unsolved mysteries, though it is claimed he died in Nepal in 1859.

# 14 ✥ Preparing for Battle

Rani Lakshmibai had been kept well informed by her agents about the advance of the British forces. She was already preoccupied at that time, battling both her neighbours Datia and Orchha, who were still trying to extract whatever advantage they could from the situation. However, after some initial setbacks, she had managed to overcome both by early March.

The queen had developed a good sense of the requirements of successful warfare by now. She knew that the British had halted in Sagar to re-equip themselves. The rulers of Datia and Orchha were also laying up supplies for them. She decided to adopt the 'scorched earth' policy—destroy everything to make things difficult for the advancing army—and her forces captured most of the provisions along with some artillery. To make it even more challenging for the enemy, she got the vegetables and crops growing in the countryside around Jhansi harvested and sent to the city. Grass was cut down too, or burnt, so that there would be no fodder for the animals. Similarly, trees were chopped down, so there would be no firewood or cover left for the enemy. According to a folk song:

> *Fell the trees,*
> *commanded the Rani of Jhansi*
> *Lest the firangis hang*
> *our soldiers on them*
> *So the coward British*
> *may not be able to shout:*
> *'Hang them! Hang them in the trees!'*
> *so that in the hot sun*
> *They may have no shade!*

She prepared the city, too, for the coming battle. Jhansi's walls presented a formidable challenge to any besieging army, and they were further strengthened and repaired. Several gates opened out from them, the most important being the Orchha, Datia, Sainwar, Bhander, Lachhmi, Khanderao, Unnao and Sagar gates. All these had a tower and broad ramparts on either side with enough space for soldiers to manoeuvre during an attack. The Sagar, Orchha and Sainwar gates were specially reinforced.

When she sent out a call for volunteers, thousands poured in to join the army. The cannons were made ready and one of her best gunners, Lalubhau Bakshi, who was appointed head of ammunitions, directed to step up manufacture. According to a report:

'Six large guns have been manufactured; carriages to hold these and old guns are in the course of construction. About 200 maunds (about 7.5 tons) of saltpetre (for the manufacture of gunpowder) purchased in the Gwalior district has been brought into the fort.'

The granaries were stocked to full capacity and flour, sugar, ghee and other provisions stored at the Ganesh temple. Water supply did not pose a great problem, since the city had many wells—one inside the fort, seven in the palace, and twelve scattered within the city. Most of the silver was melted down to make currency. Lakshmibai was hard-pressed for funds, but did not hesitate to sell her jewellery and take loans to organize an effective defence. While priests offered prayers and special ceremonies were performed to ensure victory for Jhansi, messengers carried requests for aid to her old companions, Tantya Tope and Nana's nephew, Rao Sahib.

Lakshmibai personally selected the spots where the guns would be placed, along with her commander-in-chief Jawahar Singh and chief gunner Ghulam Ghaus Khan. Ghulam Ghaus supervised the placement of the different guns—Bhawani Shankar, Ghanagarj, Karakbijli, Naldar, Arjun, Samudrasamhar and others. They expected the enemy attack to come from the south, and Ghulam Ghaus planned to man the southern tower with Ghanagarj.

As author Sir John Smythe wrote in his book *Rebellious Rani:*

*How this well brought up Hindu lady could have learned so much of the fundamentals of war is one of the mysteries that shroud her personality.*

Her expertise as a military commander continued to be a source of great wonder to her opponents. Like Joan of Arc, she had a flair for military leadership and seemed to know instinctively the right course to pursue, better than most of the other more experienced rebel leaders.

While she was ready to face the opponents, she continued to dispatch letters to Sir Robert Hamilton and Commissioner W.C. Erskine at the same time, trying her best to avoid war.

Lakshmibai had not taken the decision to go into open battle with the British impulsively or on her own. She had discussed the matter over and over again with her advisers—her father Moropant, Jawahar Singh, Raghunath Singh, Dewan Lakshman Rao Bande, her other ministers and the Bundela chieftains. The leading citizens of the city as well as the leaders of the remaining sepoys were consulted, too.

Opinions were divided. Moropant, Jawahar Singh and the other Thakurs wanted to fight, while others like Lalubhau Bakshi and some ministers advocated peace. The former felt that after their successful combat against Orchha and Datia, they could well withstand the British.

Raja Mardan Singh and Bakhtab Ali of Shahgarh appeared in Jhansi on 15 March. This was just five days before the British arrived. Mardan Singh was accompanied by his son Sher Singh and a force of 2,500 cavalry and infantry, along with two guns. More discussions followed, but without any conclusive outcome. Then the two rajas set off for Kalpi, which was occupied by Tantya Tope at that time.

The queen had made up her mind to fight, by now. She felt it was more important to save her honour rather than her life. Better still, she received news that Tantya was coming to her help with an army of 25,000 men. On 16 March, she moved into the palace within the fort, while her father Moropant stayed back in the city palace.

Once the decision was made, the Rani announced it to the people of Jhansi. She asked everyone to assemble in the town square and arrived on an elephant, dressed for battle in male attire. Damodar accompanied her. She addressed them, saying that the British army was advancing against Jhansi, so they should fight for their motherland against the foreign invader. She also informed them about the preparations and exhorted them to stand firm against the enemy.

The citizens of Jhansi responded with enthusiasm. They burst into loud cheers and cries of *'Rani Lakshmibai ki jai!'* and *'Jhansi Raj ki jai!'*

But how could it be possible to fill each and every heart with the same fervour? There was already a good amount of scepticism from some citizens. Lakshmibai heard that some of the wealthy inhabitants were transferring money and sending their families to Gwalior for safety. If the situation went out of hand, it could lead to panic. Something had to be done to restore confidence.

The Rani got an excellent idea. The festival of haldi-kumkum, observed by women, was approaching. She decided to celebrate it in a grander style than ever and invited as many women from the city as possible, regardless of caste, creed or social position. On the day concerned, a stream of women headed for the palace, colourfully dressed in their best saris and jewellery. The wealthy ones came in style, in elegant palanquins, escorted by attendants in uniform. Others, like Jhalkari Bai and her companions, simply walked in, and they all received an equally warm welcome from the queen.

A magnificent image of the goddess Gauri, decked with fabulous diamond jewellery, was placed in the durbar hall. The hall itself was richly decorated, with brocade curtains, the finest carpets and dazzling chandeliers. Garlands of flowers, looped around the walls, added their fragrance. At least a hundred maids went around with silver trays offering the guests haldi-kumkum—turmeric and vermilion powder—sandalwood paste, flowers and sweets. The festivities began at two in the afternoon and continued till nine at night.

This celebration did a lot to reassure the citizens of Jhansi that the queen was very much in control and confident of her success in the approaching battle.

Indeed, apart from strengthening her defences and stocking up for a siege, Lakshmibai had taken all the measures possible for the city's security. It was important to have knowledge of the enemy's movements. Hence all the villages surrounding Jhansi were asked to follow an old system of passing on information. When they caught sight of the British troops, they would light a fire on a hillock. Seeing the signal, the next village would follow suit and so on. In this way the news of the British advance reached long before they actually arrived.

Lakshmibai was in touch with Tantya Tope and Rao Sahib, who were now at a close distance from Jhansi, along with their forces. Tantya launched a sudden attack on two British allies, the rulers of Panna and Charkhari. He conquered the fort of Charkhari and acquired twenty-four guns and extracted a sum of Rs 3 lakh from the raja. This is when he received the Rani's appeal for help.

In the meantime Lord Canning had ordered Hugh Rose and Robert Hamilton to go and shore up the British supporters at Panna and Charkhari. Rose was only 22.5 km away from Jhansi at that time. He felt it would make more sense to conquer Jhansi first, which was considered the most important rebel stronghold at that time, and Hamilton was of the same opinion. Hugh Rose himself wrote that Jhansi was 'the strongest fortress in central India'. This fort was considered almost impregnable and originally the Supreme Command had suggested that Rose avoid Jhansi and go to Kalpi instead. After some discussion, the two decided to sidestep the governor-general's orders. Brigadier C.S. Stuart, who had set out from Mhow following a route further north but parallel to Rose's, had conquered the fort of Chanderi and was now turning towards Jhansi, so it seemed a better plan of action.

## Why Tantya 'Tope'?

Apparently Tantya Tope acquired the name 'Tope' after Bajirao II gifted him a hat or 'topi', which he always wore. His real name was Ramchandra Pandurang; Tantya was a pet name.

Tantya Tope's descendants still live in Kanpur. When the 150th anniversary of the First War of Independence was being celebrated in 2007, his third-generation descendant Vinayak Rao Tope, who was living in poverty, received a grant of Rs 1 lakh from the government and a promise of future assistance.

# 15 ❋ The Siege

It was the month of March, when the heat is gathering strength and dust-laden winds begin to tear dry leaves from the trees. Rose reached Jhansi on 20 March and took stock of the situation. Some historians say that the British offered to parley at first. Vishnu Godse, a Brahmin priest present during the siege, talks about a letter asking the Rani to come and meet 'the captain', possibly Sir Robert Hamilton, along with eight ministers, but without an armed escort. This offer was apparently turned down. It sounded too much like a trap; though it is possible that some negotiations took place, which failed.

As a highly experienced general, Rose had studied the city before him in detail. In a dispatch dated 30 April 1858, he mentions the strong points of the fort: 'It stands on an elevated rock, rising out of the plain, and commands the city and its surrounding country. It is built of excellent and most massive masonry . . .' He thus realized the difficulty of breaching its granite walls, sixteen to twenty feet thick.

The fort had elaborate outworks for artillery, and the guns placed on its turrets could target spots all around. The city lay around the fort, except on the west and part of the south. The steep rock protected the west, and the city wall ended in a small, rounded hillock in the south-east. This mound was also a strategic point for defence, being manned with five guns and partly surrounded by a twelve-feet-deep ditch. The city walls were themselves six to twelve feet thick and mounted with a variety of artillery.

Thus Jhansi was well fortified on all sides. Rose felt that the mound on the south presented the best opportunity to penetrate the city, which would have to be occupied before they could attack the fort. His aim was to batter down a portion of the wall from this position. The gates had been barricaded with piles of rocks and were strongly defended, so it would not be easy to enter through them. He gave orders to Brigadier Stuart to surround Jhansi with his cavalry and set up seven 'Flying Camps of Cavalry' to prevent anyone from escaping from the city. This is what had happened during their earlier engagements en route to Jhansi.

Reports say that the first shot was fired from the city on the evening of 21 March. The British were still waiting for the heavy siege guns to arrive from Chanderi. On 23 March, however, they launched a massive assault on the hillock. The battle that followed was fierce beyond measure. But Lakshmibai's gunners gave as well as they got. The defenders had thirteen batteries and about thirty to forty cannons. Ghulam Ghaus Khan, the chief gunner, and Khuda Baksh, another expert artilleryman, kept up a relentless rain of fire on the attackers. The Rani would ride along the rampart encouraging her soldiers, giving orders. Some of the women soldiers like Mandar manned the batteries, too, or kept the gunners supplied with ammunition. The moment a gun was disabled, they quickly got to work repairing it. Ghanagarj, the smokeless cannon, created most of the problems for the British. Sir Hugh later wrote:

> *The chief of the rebel artillery was a first-rate artilleryman . . . The manner in which the rebels served their guns, repaired their defences and reopened fire from batteries and guns repeatedly shut up was remarkable. From some batteries they returned shot for shot . . . Everything indicated a general and remarkable resistance.*

All the same, Jhansi was hard-pressed. On 23 March, some piles of grass caught fire in the city and caused panic. Around noon that day, the Jhansi guns fell silent. The next day, however, they were back in action, wreaking havoc among the enemy. Then on 25 March, the heavy siege guns, including two twenty-four-pound mortars, arrived from Chanderi. Hugh Rose began to pound the south tower of the city from batteries placed on the west, south and east. But the walls were so strong and thick that they could not do too much damage.

Intense firing continued from both sides, with the besieged army suffering heavy losses despite their determination. The red cannon balls glowed menacingly as they curved over the city walls, striking terror into the hearts of the inhabitants. Houses crumbled and fires flared up, driving people from their homes. On 26 March, the attack on the south gate was so relentless that it was impossible to retaliate. The city was filled with cries of the wounded and the bereaved. People huddled together, wondering how they could escape the enemy's fury. To make matters worse, food and water became scarce. When news came that the west wall had been breached, it created great panic.

Lakshmibai immediately mounted her horse and went around the city. She ordered her men to put out fires, comforted the frightened people and distributed food. Returning to the fort, she immediately made for Ghulam Ghaus's post.

'We must disable the attack from the west,' she said. 'One-fourth of the city is already in shambles.'

'Bai Sahiba, if you could send someone to manage the guns on the south, I'll handle the one on the west,' the gunner replied with folded hands.

'Shall I send Motibai?'

'The Bakshin might be better.'

Lalubhau Bakshi's wife manned Ghanagarj and a gun called its 'little sister'. Ghulam Ghaus Khan hurried to the west gate, where a gunner named Lalta was on duty. He examined the enemy lines closely with binoculars and realized that their guns had been concealed behind mounds of red earth.

'I know what we need to do, Lalta,' he said exultantly, turning his sights on the heaps. Within minutes the guns blew up, along with their operators. Lakshmibai had also been watching the battle through her binoculars. She summoned Ghulam Ghaus, praised him profusely for his expertise and rewarded him with gold jewellery.

This brought temporary respite to the city.

The British had nicknamed Ghanagarj as 'Whistling Dick'. When Rose heard that their guns had been silenced in the west, he ordered Stuart to go and take charge at once. Then he asked the commander in the south to step up the attack in order to put 'Whistling Dick' out of commission.

In the meantime the Bakshin was wreaking havoc on the enemy forces in the south. Gunpowder and smoke had blackened her face; sweat streaked it, while her body ached with the rigorous exertion it had undergone. But she continued to pound the British doggedly till a cannon ball crashed through the parapets and landed on her. The Bakshin fell at her post as blood started streaming from her battered body. When the queen heard this, she hurried to the spot. Lalubhau Bakshi was busy on the eastern tower. Somehow, he swallowed his grief and said, 'We will cremate her in the evening.' He went on loading, firing, reloading his gun and firing again like an automaton.

The Rani embraced her friend's fallen body and wept. Mandar ran to her, but Ghulam Ghaus said, 'Bai Sahiba, how many will you mourn? The Bakshin has gained immortality.'

Lakshmibai wiped her tears and rose as Ghulam Ghaus took charge of Ghanagarj. The battle continued, with large numbers falling on each side. On the tenth day of the siege, the western wall was breached again.

The British forces advanced, hoping to take advantage, but were repelled by a force led by the valiant Sagar Singh, a former dacoit who had been rehabilitated by the queen. He was killed, but the city was saved. The Rani dashed to the spot and supervised the repairs. By morning the wall was as good as new.

★ ★ ★

The British had not expected such a spirited defence. The women's contribution astonished them in particular. They were everywhere—manning guns, helping to repair the broken walls and doing whatever could be done to save the city. All the same, the constant battering was taking its toll on Jhansi's protectors.

On 29 March, Khudabaksh Khan was hit while manning the Sainwar gate of the city. Raghunath Singh bore the dying hero back on his horse to the fort. Seated on the threshold of the palace, the iron-hearted queen wept.

According to a folk song, Khudabaksh Khan's last words were:

> *We have to die one day, brother and*
> *I shall choose today*
> *For our queen I shall lay down my life.*
> *I shall hack the firangi with my sword*
> *And the world will forever remember me!*

If this were not enough, a grim-faced Ramchandra Deshmukh arrived on the scene. For a moment he seemed to hesitate. Then he took a deep breath and blurted out, 'Bai Sahiba, Ghulam Ghaus Khan has fallen to the enemy fire.'

Lakshmibai stared at him incredulously. Then she sprang up and said, 'Send Bhau in his place. And bring his body here. Come with me Mandar . . .'

A grave had already been dug for Khudabaksh, and Lakshmibai headed for that place. Motibai waited there, stone-faced.

'Moti,' said the queen gently. 'The cannon on the south is silent. Will you man it for a while? We are waiting to perform Ghulam Ghaus's last rites.'

'Has he gone, too?' Moti's eyes streamed. Then she pressed her fists into her eyes and made for the south tower.

But she was not meant to remain there for long. The moment she fired her first volley, a hail of bullets greeted her. She immediately collapsed on the ground.

The three of them were buried close to each other, with Gul Muhammad, the leader of the queen's loyal vilayatis, performing the last rites.

A platform was hurriedly constructed and still stands in the Jhansi Fort. To this day prayers are recited and chadars offered to these three brave souls every year on 29 March. Some accounts state, however, that the three were killed on 4 April.

Conditions were becoming desperate inside the city now. To encourage her troops, the Rani made rounds of all the battle stations and rewarded the soldiers with money and jewellery. On 30 March, the British shot at the water reservoir and destroyed it. Rose found his ammunition running low, however, and decided to send men to scale the walls, while keeping up relentless fire on the breached wall.

Inside Jhansi, the queen was wondering why her ally Tantya Tope had not arrived to support her as promised. On 31 March, the eleventh day of the siege, morale was plummeting severely when a lookout on the tower of the fort cried out, 'The Peshwa's army!' Others took up the cry. The Rani, Moropant and Jawahar Singh hurried to the main tower and drank in the sight through their binoculars.

Dusk was falling, but it was unmistakably Tantya's army that they glimpsed on the banks of the Betwa river. Tantya had lit a huge bonfire, which burned like a beacon of hope for the beleaguered citizens of Jhansi. There was general rejoicing in the city that had been brought to its edge by all the preceding days and nights of tension.

Rose's situation was unenviable at that moment. He had not been able to break through the queen's defences and now faced an assault from a force of 22,000 soldiers. The news had reached him beforehand via telegraph; and seasoned soldier that he was, he wasted no time in planning his defence. He left some troops around Jhansi and dispatched the rest in different directions. Some were to remain hidden on both sides of the Kalpi–Jhansi road. Others were sent ten miles to the north to man the hills near Garhmau lake. Another group took up their posts next to the Orchha road.

Tantya kept the larger portion of his army with him in Betwa and divided the rest into three parts, which were sent towards Jhansi via Garhmau. He swooped down on the British at 4 a.m., hoping to take them by surprise. At first he maintained his advantage, flanking the enemy from both sides. Then Rose, who was heavily outnumbered, attacked with his cavalry and horse artillery from both right and left in full force. While Tantya had plenty of ammunition and artillery, apart from the rebel sepoys of the Gwalior contingent, Naoganj and Kanpur, the Nawab of Banda's and the Banpur and Shahgarh forces, his troops consisted mostly of ill-trained peasants equipped with old-fashioned matchlocks, which did not stand a chance against the British Enfield. The sepoys and the vilayatis or Afghan mercenaries fought bravely till the last, but some of the raw recruits took to their heels, causing confusion. Seeing that the day was lost, Tantya set fire to the surrounding jungle and retreated across the Betwa to Kalpi. He was able to save the major part of his army as well as some guns. Most of his ammunition, however, along with eighteen guns, was lost to the British as also some elephants and camels.

In the meantime, within the city, the queen and her advisers had noted that the barrage of fire from the besieging force had lessened in intensity. They kept up their own assault, but confident that the worst was over and Tantya would save the day for them, they did not make any attempts to venture out and strike the depleted British force.

When the course of the battle went against Tantya, the mood became grimmer than ever. But the Rani quickly pulled herself together and addressed her forces. 'Tantya has retreated, but that does not mean we should lose hope. We are strong enough to fight for our motherland and send the goras back. If anyone here fears for their lives, they are free to leave. The rest of us will fight as long as we draw breath. If we have to die, we will die with honour, not let the goras slaughter us like cattle.'

Not a single man or woman budged. Lakshmibai made rounds of the city, stopping to talk to an old woman here or a prosperous merchant there, while puris were cooked and distributed to the troops.

Motibai, Sundar, Lalubhau Bakshi and all the others manned their guns with renewed fervour. On the night of 2 April, the assault on the city was unbearable. The British fire rained relentlessly and not a soul slept in Jhansi. The queen was constantly on the move—encouraging the gunners and distributing rewards to those who performed extra well. Then suddenly a very loud explosion startled her. It came from the direction of the Khas Mahal, the main palace in the fort. When she went to investigate along with Dewan Jawahar Singh, she found that the palace had been hit and the Ganesha temple destroyed. Some of the Brahmins took shelter in the basement, along with other men and women.

The Jhansi gunners turned their cannons towards the direction from which the fire had come. Soon the

British guns fell silent and the hard-pressed people took a breather.

But this respite was short-lived. The constant battering had taken a toll on the mound, and the breach was large enough for the British to make a concerted assault. On the morning of 3 April, they stormed the city from both left and right. While one party kept up the firing on the left to distract attention, another was deputed to scale the walls furtively from the right. It was a bright moonlit night and the plan to enter the city without being detected did not work. The defenders saw the enemy advancing, the queen's bugle blew and torches lit up all over the fort, exposing the invasion. They rained cannon balls, live coals, stones, logs, anything they could, on those swarming up the ladders. Drums were beaten and bugles blown to frighten the enemy. When three of the ladders broke, a bugle sounded from the British side, signalling a retreat. They returned, however, with reinforcements. The troops who had already successfully broken the defence on the south came to the aid of their comrades.

It is said that a man named Dewan Dulhaju, who manned the Orchha gate, betrayed the queen. He directed his fire away from the enemy, indicated the weaker points and even opened the gate. The valiant Sundar tried to stop him, but was slain by the traitor. The British later rewarded Dewan Dulhaju with grants of land.

A large number of men and four British officers—Dick, Meikle John, Bonus and Fox—lost their lives in the second attempt to scale the city walls. Dilip Singh

Pawar, a thakur from Orchha, killed them but fell to their bullets, unfortunately. According to the account left by Vishnu Godse, Rose's army used not only ladders but also bundles of grass.

Now the enemy was inside the city, dealing out death and destruction. The Rani witnessed the terrible scenes of pillage through her binoculars from the heights of the citadel. For a moment she sat down to think, then rose and summoned the leaders—Jawahar Singh, Raghunath Singh, Gul Muhammad, Lalubhau Bakshi, Nana Bhopatkar and others.

'It is time to go out and fight,' she said. 'We have to drive the enemy from the city!'

There was no time for discussion and debate. Sword in hand, Lakshmibai burst out, followed by 1,500 soldiers—both Pathans and Bundelas. She swept through the city like a fury, stunning the invaders with the ferocity of her attack. She even took on her foes in hand to hand fights and felled large numbers with her own blade. Many of the British troops retreated and took shelter inside houses to escape her. Bullets whizzed past, fires blazed up and the cries of the injured filled the air. The Rani was the main target. The enemy knew that once she fell, the defence of the city would fall apart. Suddenly an elderly chief appeared before her. 'Bai Sahiba,' he pleaded, 'take my life, but please don't expose yourself like this. We all depend on you. The fort is still in our possession; we can continue the battle from there.'

Gul Muhammad nodded his approval and the Rani was persuaded to return to the fort. Only 300 Afghans could return with her. The rest fell fighting, along with the Bundelas.

Jhansi was not conquered easily. There was fierce resistance. The British might have been out to destroy the city, but its defenders fought for each and every inch. The palace witnessed an intense conflict. About thirty of the queen's devoted bodyguards stood till the end, trying to hold on to the stables, hitting out with swords in both hands and firing back even when they had been gunned down. When the stables were set on fire, they rushed out with their clothes in flames, still striking out at the enemy. All of them lost their lives, but managed to kill and wound many more.

### The Durga Dal

The Rani's Durga Dal of women warriors has often been compared to the mythical Amazons. When Subhas Chandra Bose founded the Indian National Army in 1943, he created a Rani of Jhansi regiment for women fighters.

## 16 ❋ Escape!

The scene was such that it would have plunged the bravest into despair. Standing in the fort, Lakshmibai could get a clear view of the carnage. She could see the flames, smell the smoke and, over the booming of the guns, hear the cries of her beloved subjects as they suffered the full force of the enemy's brutality. Against Rose's orders, numberless women and children were slaughtered. Many jumped into wells to escape dishonour. Gold and silver ornaments, cash, household goods and anything worth robbing was taken from the houses. The idols in the temples were desecrated, their jewellery pillaged. The palace was torched, along with its magnificent furnishings, including the theatre and all the props lovingly accumulated by Gangadhar Rao. When the queen saw flames shoot up from the library with all its precious manuscripts, it became too much for her to bear. Her head swam and she would have fallen down if Mandar, who was nearby, had not supported her. She quickly sent for water. The Rani sipped it, with tears flowing unchecked down her cheeks as she continued to witness Jhansi's tragedy.

The southern part had been taken over. The prosperous locality of Halwaipura was being looted by the conquerors, while the dwellings of the Koris, too, were in flames.

Then the Rani seemed to come to some kind of a decision. She retired to splash some water on her exhausted frame, put on fresh clothes and gathered everyone together. 'The enemy has occupied the city, and could be here any moment now,' she said. 'Those of us who do not die fighting will be caught and hanged. Even if I die, I cannot think of tolerating the dishonour of an Englishman touching my corpse. I've decided to blow myself up with gunpowder, so no trace of my body remains.'

For a moment all were stunned into silence. Then an elderly sardar spoke, 'Bai Sahiba, you will commit suicide? You know very well that it's a sin. And what about Damodar? Who will take care of him? If you manage to get away right now, you can try to reach Kalpi and join up with the Peshwa's forces. Together you can continue the struggle for swarajya.'

Lakshmibai flushed and her eyes dropped. She said in a low voice, 'Baba, you have shown me the way. I will fight. Friends . . . please overlook this moment of weakness.' She continued briskly, 'We have to get ready to leave. Those who cannot do battle must escape through the secret tunnel. The rest of us will go out through the Bhanderi gate. Who will take charge of it?'

A Kori fighter was deputed for the task, and he left through one of the secret doors of the fort, it is said. Lalubhau would divert the enemy's attention by continuing to keep Karakbijli spitting fire from the eastern tower of the fort.

It was the night of 4 April. A little before midnight, when the moon was supposed to rise, the Rani got ready to leave. She distributed money and gifts to her old retainers. They touched her feet and left, weeping. Then she donned her armour, wore an angarakha over it and put a turban on her head. She placed two loaded revolvers in her cummerbund, along with a sword. Then she mounted her favourite horse, Sarangi. Damodar sat behind her, tied to her back with a silk sash. Jawahar Singh, Raghunath Singh, Mandar, Gul Muhammad and 300 vilayatis and twenty-five other horsemen accompanied her. They stepped out through a door on the northern side where the stables lay. Gold and jewellery had been distributed among all the queen's companions. They carried it in bags tied to their waists.

Her father Moropant retained some of the remaining troops and left later. He was, however, eventually captured by the British, as was Lalubhau Bakshi. Moropant's wife Chimabai had already crept out of the city with her infant son and managed to reach her father's place at Gursarai safely.

In the beginning the Rani and her troops rode through parts of the city still unoccupied by the British. Hundreds of Lakshmibai's subjects paused in the midst of their desperate attempts to save themselves and bid her farewell. Slowly and silently the party disappeared into the darkness. The Kori was waiting. He opened the Bhanderi gate swiftly, and they slipped out.

> *This gate remained shut for seventy-five years and was only reopened in the winter of 1933.*

But three rows of soldiers, British and some from Orchha, had been stationed outside each gate. When they challenged the defenders, saying, 'Who goes there?' Lakshmibai replied in the Bundelkhandi dialect, making her voice low and masculine, 'We're from Orchha—soldiers.'

They continued at an even pace till they had passed the British camps, laughing and joking to lull any doubts that they were just a bunch of loyal troops. Then they quickened their pace and separated into groups.

The Rani sped through the night along with her people. Soon Rose discovered that his prey had slipped out of his reach. For a while the British were misled when Jhalkari, a member of the Rani's Durga Dal, rode through the streets dressed like the queen. She was caught and taken to the general's camp where the ruse was discovered. Rose immediately asked the cavalry to pursue the queen. Tantya had received news of her escape, too, and sent out men to help her. 34 km from Jhansi, near the village of Bhander, Lieutenant Dowker of the Hyderabad Cavalry caught sight of her. He gave chase and was gaining on her, when she turned and slashed him with her sword. Had it not been for the revolver on his hip, he would have been cut into two. His companions came to his assistance, but in the meantime

Lakshmibai and her attendants got away. She reached Kalpi on 5 April, having covered 163 km of extremely rough terrain in twenty-four hours.

The queen managed to escape, but Jhansi had to bear the full brunt of British vandalism. First it was the British troops that plundered the houses of all the valuables they could lay their hands on—gold, silver, even statues of the gods. The palace was stripped of all its treasures—the diamonds from Panna, the Burma rubies and other invaluable jewels. The furnishings and even the rare manuscripts in the library that escaped the fire were ruthlessly torn apart. After the white men were done with this, it was the turn of the Indian troops from Madras and Hyderabad to lay their hands on whatever remained: the brass and copper utensils; even clothes and grain were not spared.

Veterinary surgeon Sylvester, writing in *Recollections of the Campaign in Malwa and Central India*, remembered:

> One class of articles, however, seemed to me to be looked on as fair loot even by the most scrupulous—these were the gods found in the temples. They were collected in great numbers, and were strangely sought after by every officer and soldier. There were Gunputties and Vishnoos innumerable, and of every metal.

People were desperate to save themselves in the city, which was turning into one vast cremation ground. Vishnu Godse has written that his host, Keshav Bhat, informed him about broad recesses built in the thick walls of a nearby mansion, accessible through a tunnel. As the gunfire crept closer and closer to their house, they hurried into these hiding places. They found them already crammed with people seeking safety. Terrified, they crouched there, trying not to think of the ghastly scenes that were being enacted outside.

Amnesty was declared on the eighth day. When the survivors stepped out cautiously, the scenes of devastation tore at their hearts. It seemed there was hardly a building that remained untouched. Worse, hundreds of corpses were piled up in the streets and an unbearable stench filled the once magnificent city.

### How did the Rani escape Jhansi?

According to legend, the Rani, mounted on Sarangi, leapt from the fort, with Damodar tied to her back, and escaped the British. Anyone who has visited Jhansi Fort knows it would be impossible to do this and survive. Yet, this story continues to fascinate people and she has often been depicted as jumping from the wall in illustrations and friezes.

# 17 ✳ At Kalpi

Lakshmibai's headlong flight ended when she reached Kalpi at 2 a.m. This city lay to the north-east of Jhansi on the banks of the Jamuna river. It possessed a well-built fort and had passed back and forth from Maratha to British rule. It acquired the status of a major rebel stronghold when the troops stationed here supported the sepoys who arrived from Kanpur. For this reason, Nana Sahib's nephew, Rao Sahib, decided to camp here with his army.

The queen received a courteous welcome. But though physically exhausted, her troubled mind could not be at rest. She retired to a tent with Damodar and Mandar, and spent a restless night. The next morning she met the Peshwa's nephew.

Her arrival there was a matter of embarrassment for Rao Sahib. He was partly responsible for the Rani's predicament. If his army had not been routed near the Betwa river, she might have still been secure in her own kingdom.

Dejected and simmering with rage, Lakshmibai maintained her poise outwardly. She greeted Rao Sahib politely, then took her sword out of its scabbard and placed it at his feet. 'Your noble forefathers honoured our family by presenting this sword to us, so we could protect our people. Now that we seem to have lost your goodwill, I request you to take it back.'

Rao Sahib flushed. He gazed down at the sword, then cleared his throat and said, 'I know ... we failed to provide you with proper support in your struggle. But you challenged the might of the British with unbelievable courage. The whole country resounds with praise for your valour.' He paused and glanced at the queen's taut face. There was a pleading note in his voice as he went on. 'You know that the Holkars and Scindias are no longer on our side. Now, more than ever, we need leaders like you to keep up the resistance. I beg you, please do not surrender the sword.'

It was a deeply charged moment.

The tension dissipated when Lakshmibai picked up the sword. Her large eyes shot sparks as she said, 'I am ready to offer my life for our cause. What could be nobler than dying to save the motherland?'

Tantya Tope was already there. Her old allies Mardan Singh, the Raja of Banpur, Bakhtab Ali, the Raja of Shahgarh and the Nawab of Banda were busy raising armies and would arrive shortly. But when the Rani inspected the troops, she realized that even though they had numbers, the motley crew before her could hardly be considered a match for the well-trained British troops. There were some rebel sepoys—soldiers from the Gwalior army, the Kotah cavalry and the remnants of the Jhansi forces. The rest, however, were peasants who had not received any military training or robbers and thieves who had joined in the hope of opportunities for looting. Time was extremely short and they had to try and organize these disparate elements into an efficient fighting force. To make matters worse, while Rao Sahib paid heed to her advice, some of the other commanders felt that as a mere woman her opinion should not be given too much weight. This made it very hard to create and implement a consistent battle plan.

They had received information that Rose had made arrangements to secure Jhansi and was on his way to fight the rebels. By the third week of April, all their supporters had arrived in Kalpi. Lakshmibai was of the view that instead of holing up there, they should engage the enemy at Krunch, a town 70 km away. Its topography had better scope for an effective resistance: forests and temples surrounded the town, making the approach difficult for an attacking army.

The battle took place on 7 May, and was a short one. The Peshwa's army was routed once again, even though the heat took a strong toll on the white forces. Tantya, who believed in the traditional style of facing the enemy head on, ignored the Rani's advice to cover his flanks instead of concentrating his forces in the centre. The master strategist, Hugh Rose, had on the other hand divided his troops into three columns. While the central one was engaging the rebel army, more men closed in on both sides, supported by heavy artillery. Outmanoeuvred, Tantya's men were forced to retreat. They stood their ground as long as they could, even inflicted terrible casualties with their swords, but had to ultimately abandon the field and save themselves.

Tantya fled to Chirkhi, a village that lay 30 km away, close to where his parents stayed; Lakshmibai returned to Kalpi. A bitter post mortem of the battle took place. Not only the commanders, but the soldiers, too, traded accusations. Demoralized, a lot of them abandoned their posts and left. Rumours of a fresh British assault created panic and it seemed all was lost, when the Nawab of Banda arrived with an army of 2,000 cavalry, several guns and a large train of animals and ammunition. Hope was revived and many of the deserters returned, mostly because of the Rani's popularity. While Rao Sahib was nominally the commander-in-chief, everyone knew Lakshmibai was the real leader.

Hugh Rose set off for Kalpi on 9 May at 2 a.m. The victorious army was in a terrible shape. The white soldiers found the heat unbearable, and longed for shade and water, both hard to find. The general was short of ammunition, too. For this reason Colonel Maxwell was sent to support him with a column of the Bengal Army.

Both the commanders knew that Kalpi would not be an easy conquest. While it had a well-built fort, the labyrinth of ravines that surrounded it formed its main defence. They were overgrown with shrubs and made a natural hiding place for troops. Moreover, the Rani had reinforced this geographical protection by adding trenches and barricades. At least eighty-four temples and graveyards lay around the city, too, affording greater protection against any attack.

Sir Hugh's spies had informed him about all these obstacles; hence the general evolved his strategy accordingly. He moved his forces to the east towards the Jamuna river and halted at the village of Golauli, about 5 km from Kalpi. This spot had open terrain, which would make it easier for him to use his manpower and artillery to the best effect.

On receiving the news, Lakshmibai, in turn, outmanoeuvred him by attacking from the rear. The British were in a tight position, but managed to hold on. The Peshwa's army tried to draw them into the ravines, but Rose decided to play the waiting game. He wanted to join Colonel Maxwell, who was waiting on the opposite side of the Jamuna with his forces. Without the support of the colonel's camel corps, he could not make an effective assault on Kalpi. Other problems plagued him, too—a severe shortage of drinking water, fresh vegetables for his ailing troops and fodder for the horses. As a folk song goes:

> *With tears in his eyes*
> *Proud Hugh Rose spoke:*
> *'I beg you for one pot of water*
> *To quench my thirst,'*
> *The reply came: 'To get that potful*
> *You must hand over your guns*
> *Your ammunition and your sword as well!'*

The Indians had removed all the boats from the river to prevent Maxwell from crossing over. Rose had to send for ferries from Poona, and the two commanders were finally able to meet on 17 May. The Indian army had been maintaining pressure by drawing the enemy into small skirmishes. There was, however, no major engagement till 20 May, when the Rani launched a strong assault on their right flank and caused heavy casualties. But Rose moved in more troops and ordered his men to maintain their position, which they did. The same night Maxwell's camel corps crossed the Jamuna and brought further reinforcements.

Lakshmibai had been drilling the soldiers, tirelessly, to keep them fit for battle. Consequently she was taken aback when, on 21 May, Rao Sahib decided that she would not lead the army. He himself would act as commander-in-chief. The Gwalior troops would take orders from him. While the Nawab of Banda was to deploy his strong force of 2,000 soldiers in the south of Kalpi, the sepoys from Awadh and Rohillkhand were ordered to protect the city and the fort. Raja Mardan Singh of Banpur and his troops would guard the west along with the Shahgarh ruler, Bakhtab Ali. The Rani was left with 250 mounted soldiers—the red-shirted Afghan vilayatis—directly under her, to defend the northern side of the city. This arrangement was to affect the outcome of the battle adversely.

On 22 May, the Indians decided to strike with full force. Their strategy was that the Nawab of Banda would attack the left of the right flank of the British army first, and Rao Sahib the left centre. This would compel the right centre and other troops to come to their assistance. The queen, who would be hidden in the ravines, would emerge and launch another attack to compel the British to fall back.

This plan almost worked. Brigadier Stuart was taken in and sent a message to Hugh Rose, saying that there seemed to be no threat from the right. But the canny Hugh Rose had either found out beforehand or sensed that the silence on the right was a ploy. He deployed his troops accordingly. The infantry and some cavalry were placed on the right, facing the network of ravines; the heavy artillery formed the central line towards the south, while a combination of units were concentrated on the left, along with the camel corps which had just crossed the river during the night.

When the Nawab of Banda advanced on the left and launched a concerted attack, the British retaliated with heavy artillery fire. The Indian soldiers were initially thrown back, but the Nawab rallied them. Rao Sahib's forces made their way towards the centre. In the meantime, Hugh Rose sent one company of soldiers to the ravines, convinced that the main attack would come from there.

He was correct. The rulers of Banpur and Shahgarh had finally opted to serve with the queen, and she had been hidden there with 400 cavalry and 2,000 infantry. The soldiers were deployed in an orderly manner— infantry with guns in front, similarly armed horsemen behind them, then infantry bearing swords behind them, and finally cavalry carrying swords in the rear. As the British forces advanced, Lakshmibai burst out of the ravines. A ferocious battle ensued. Hugh Rose mentioned in a dispatch: 'The sepoy-cavalry came out of their hiding places and advanced in groups with great discipline. Only rebel after rebel was to be seen as far as the eye could see.'

Her blue turban fell off as the Rani swooped on the enemy, mounted on Sarangi, waving her sword. Her cry of 'Har-Har Mahadev!' rallied all the Indian soldiers and struck fear into the hearts of her opponents. Brigadier Stuart's horse was killed under him as they fought. Most of the British troops fell, many horses were lost and the day would have gone very badly for them if Rose had not appeared with 700 soldiers of the camel division along with Major Ross, the officer commanding them. They almost surrounded Lakshmibai, but her Afghans saved her and bore her away. Unfortunately, she lost her much-loved steed Sarangi in this battle.

The Nawab of Banda was in trouble, too, but he continued to battle on, waiting for Rao Sahib to come to his support. But the commander-in-chief had made for the west with his Gwalior contingent. The Nawab was thus forced to retreat. He was daring enough to return to Kalpi that night and direct the remaining troops to abandon the city. He remained there till daybreak, overseeing operations, when Brigadier Stuart surprised him on his way out. The Nawab had to flee, abandoning ten cannons.

Hugh Rose entered the city and found it deserted. A huge store of arms was part of the booty that fell to the captors.

The Rani did not go back. She went westwards, too, and it is said that there was a bitter encounter with the feckless Rao Sahib on the way. She had had to leave in such haste that she spent the night under a tree.

The British celebrated their victory, which they firmly believed was a decisive one. Hugh Rose relaxed and looked forward to some respite from the rigours of campaigning. But little did they know that the chapter was not closed as yet.

## The Nawab of Banda

The Nawab of Banda or Ali Bahadur II was a descendant of the legendary couple Peshwa Baji Rao I and his beautiful Muslim wife Mastani. He was one of the few of the queen's supporters fortunate enough to escape execution by the British, perhaps because he was not accused of killing civilians.

After the defeat at Gwalior, he returned to his kingdom to battle on and was eventually defeated by General Whitlock. He was exiled to Indore and awarded a pension of Rs 36,000 per annum.

# 18 🌀 An Audacious Plan

It was a downcast and desperate group that met again at Gopalpur, a town that lay at a distance of 74 km to the south-west of Gwalior. Disillusioned, seething with fury at her allies' incompetence, the Rani had ridden for several days and nights till she reached this place.

A shamefaced Tantya Tope, who had inexplicably stayed away at Chirkhi, decided to come, too. He had abandoned his friends at a crucial time and they had all been driven into a corner. Now the British would hunt them down mercilessly. They had neither army nor ammunition worth the name to put up any kind of resistance. If they wished to die with honour, they had to find a place where they could make some kind of stand. The queen suggested Bundelkhand, but Tantya felt they would not receive adequate support there. Rao Sahib wanted to head towards the Deccan, the traditional stronghold of the Peshwas. The distance was a great deterrent, however. It would be next to impossible to get there without being caught on the way.

The rebel movement was truly stuck in the doldrums when, once again, Lakshmibai came to the rescue. Her fertile brain conjured up a daring plan—to attack Gwalior and take over Jayajirao Scindia's army.

Rao Sahib and the Nawab of Banda were not in favour, but Tantya thought the idea was quite workable. He had friends in Gwalior and knew Jayajirao's troops were simmering with discontent. They felt that their ruler and his prime minister Dinkar Rao were stooges of the British and traitors to the cause.

Gwalior was the second richest and one of the most influential states of India. Young Jayajirao did not, however, possess the qualities of a strong ruler. Dinkar Rao actually ran the government, along with the British resident McPherson. When the rebellion began in northern India, Scindia spent anxious days, trying to keep his troops under control. Eventually the Gwalior contingent did leave and join Tantya Tope, but Jayajirao's 10,000-strong private army stayed with him.

When Scindia heard that Kalpi had fallen, he was elated that his allies, the British, were in control again. Soon after, he received a letter from Rao Sahib asking him to join them. Scindia immediately informed Sir Robert Hamilton. Dinkar Rao suggested that they keep up negotiations. The British were on their way in any case. Jayajirao felt the same way and agreed. In the meantime another message arrived from Rao Sahib, saying that all they wanted from the king was temporary refuge, so they could rest and recover, some financial help, and the assurance of safe passage to the Deccan.

The young ruler Jayajirao was, however, misled by one of his officers, who told him that the rebel army was in shambles and he could cover himself with glory by easily defeating them. Amirchand Bantiya, his treasurer, and other officials also egged him on, saying that he would gain highly in stature by capturing the famous Rani of Jhansi.

Scindia disregarded the more astute Dinkar Rao's advice and decided to take to the battlefield. On 1 June, he headed towards the village of Bahadurpur, where the rebels were camping, with some troops. When he came close, he fired a cannon in warning. Scindia's stance confused Rao Sahib and Tantya. They were not sure whether the presence of the soldiers and the cannon shot meant a ceremonial welcome or if the young ruler meant to attack them. The Rani took no chances. Hurriedly mustering the men, she took to the field and charged on the king of Gwalior's artillery, cutting down several gunners on the spot. Scindia's confidence ebbed. This was hardly a broken army, but he did not have much choice now.

A skirmish began. However, when Scindia's troops began to realize that the slight figure in red leading the Peshwa's army was indeed the Rani of Jhansi, they began to waver. When the rebels let out the cry of 'Deen! Deen!'—'For the faith! For the faith!'—Jayajirao's forces could not resist this call. Their leader was horrified when they deserted him and rushed over to the other side, greeting their erstwhile opponents like long lost brothers. It is said that after this they all set off together to feast on watermelons at the riverbed in Morar. The stunned Scindia had to flee for his life. He made for Dholpur, planning to head for Agra from there. So unnerved was he that he did not even halt to guarantee the safety of his womenfolk. Later, they took shelter in the Narwar fort. Dinkar Rao and other officials followed him post haste.

Lakshmibai thus saved the day for the rebels, and this has been commemorated in yet another folk song:

> From clay and stones
> She moulded her army.
> From mere wood
> She made swords
> And the mountain she transformed
>     into a steed.
> Thus she marched to Gwalior!

The triumphant army entered the city and only realized what a goldmine had fallen into their hands when they took stock of Gwalior's wealth and plenty. It was a peaceful takeover. The officers in the city's administration, who had chosen to remain behind, were confirmed in their posts. The common people did not suffer at all; only the houses of the Dewan and wealthy families like the Phadkes and Balwant Rao were plundered. According to some accounts, the treasurer Amirchand Bantiya, who was sympathetic to the rebel cause, opened the royal treasury and Scindia's soldiers were paid three months' salary, which was due to them, and two months' extra as a reward. It came to Rs 9 lakh. 7,50,000 rupees was supposedly distributed among the soldiers on the rebel side. The Nawab of Banda received 60,000, Lakshmibai 20,000, while Rao Sahib took 15,000 worth of gold coins.

This windfall had an adverse effect, however. The leaders decided to commemorate their victory in style. A grand coronation ceremony was held on 3 June 1858, at the Phoolbagh palace, with Rao Sahib assuming the jewelled turban as a representative of the Peshwa Nana Sahib. An enormous canopy, magnificently decorated, was set up to receive thousands of guests and a 101-gun salute fired. Tantya was awarded the rank of a general. Brahmins were fed for fourteen days and lakh of rupees squandered in a lavish celebration.

Sensing her disapproval perhaps, the others left the Rani out of their discussions. She received a last minute invitation on 2 June, but the revelry dismayed her. This was the time to plan future action, she believed, and her allies were frittering away precious hours in meaningless festivity. It is said that she remarked caustically that the Peshwa's representative was preparing sugar balls for the Brahmins when cannon balls were needed.

As she had anticipated, this delay had ominous consequences. The easily won victory, followed by their complacency, proved to be their downfall. Though he had stated earlier that he intended to march on to the Deccan, Rao Sahib lingered on in Gwalior, revelling in luxury instead of formulating plans for future action and consolidating his gains to the best advantage.

# Why did Rao Sahib claim to be Scindia's overlord?

The Peshwa was once the nominal overlord of the Scindias. Ranoji, the founder of the Scindia dynasty, was said to have begun his career as the slipper bearer of Peshwa Balaji Baji Rao. He rose in the Peshwa's favour because of his good qualities and was granted the right to collect taxes in certain areas of central India in 1726. In time his descendants grew in power and Gwalior became the largest state of central India. However, after the third Anglo–Maratha War, all the Maratha kingdoms, including Gwalior, Indore and Nagpur, came under British control.

# 19 Another Encounter with the General

The news that the rebels had occupied Gwalior came as a great shock to the British. Rose was making plans for his retirement, and the general belief was that the central India campaign had been successfully concluded. All that was required now, everyone felt, was to hunt down the defeated insurgents and their leaders.

This daring feat upset all their plans. Canning did not underestimate the significance of the fall of Gwalior. Till this time, the rebellion had been confined to northern India. Gwalior, with its strategic location, could easily be a stepping-stone to the south and the west. The Marathas would rally behind the Peshwa and the situation could easily spiral out of control. The monsoons would also be breaking soon, making it extremely difficult to conduct a campaign. The rivers would be in spate and the constant downpour could ruin the well-planned tactics of even the best of military commanders.

The governor-general sent out orders that a strong force should head towards Gwalior immediately. Hugh Rose left Kalpi without any further delay; Brigadier Smith was to join him from Chanderi with an entire brigade of the Rajputana Field Force. Colonel Ridell, too, was coming from Agra with infantry, cavalry and well-equipped artillery. The Hyderabad contingent, which had proved its mettle at Kalpi, was sent to man the road that led south from Gwalior.

Once again Hugh Rose devised a masterly battle plan. He aimed to first occupy the cantonment of Morar, just 8 km from Gwalior. Brigadier Smith was to be stationed twenty miles away at Kotah-ki-Sarai, a settlement that lay to the south-east of the old city of Gwalior. It would be their headquarters. The strategy was to drive the Indians into the fort by attacking from Morar and Lashkar, the new portion of the city, which was located next to the magnificent Phoolbagh palace.

On 12 June, the Indian leaders got the news that Hugh Rose was on his way. They should have expected this, but it fell on both the soldiers and their commanders like a bolt from the blue. Once again, when the situation became critical, they had no choice but to turn to the person whose advice they had consistently been ignoring.

Rao Sahib, Tantya and the Nawab of Banda went to call on the queen on 13 June. They found her seated, with Damodar on her lap. They greeted her with shamefaced looks, like a bunch of careless schoolboys who had got into a scrape.

'Bai Sahiba ... the British are coming,' Tantya said in a low voice. 'We have to face them ... as effectively as we can.'

Lakshmibai frowned. 'I am just a woman who's supposed to be ignorant of the finer points of warfare,' she replied, meeting his eyes squarely. 'But if you recall, I told you we should maintain our readiness to meet the enemy. You felt it was time to make merry. How can we hope for victory now?'

'Please, Bai Sahiba,' Tantya begged. 'You know how much faith the soldiers have in you. If you take command again, they will fight with renewed enthusiasm.'

'We have no choice whatever.' The queen gently put Damodar down and stood up. 'And if I know the general, we can't afford to waste a minute. But I will not lose heart.' She sighed, 'Ananda, my child, it's back to the warfront again for your mother.'

The young boy's eyes filled with tears, but he followed her out obediently. The faithful supporters who had come with her from Jhansi were summoned— Raghunath Singh, Gul Muhammad, Mandar, Kashi and all the others.

The queen's jaw was firmly set, but apprehension clouded her large eyes. 'I am entrusting my dearest Ananda to you,' she said. 'Who knows what the outcome of this new battle might be? I'm leaving all my money and jewellery for his upkeep. Please protect him as best you can. You know how merciless the British are. They will not spare even an innocent child.'

'Do not worry, Bai Sahiba,' Raghunath Singh said. 'We will guard him with our lives.'

★ ★ ★

Lakshmibai was to lead an army of 10,000 soldiers and they would man the Kotah-ki-Sarai front. There was very little time, but along with the Nawab of Banda, the Rani began drilling her troops.

This region teemed with ravines and gorges, providing natural cover to the defending forces. When news arrived on 15 June that Hugh Rose was barely a few miles away from Morar, Rao Sahib took up his post there with a large number of mounted soldiers and cannons. As the general's army advanced towards Morar, Rao Sahib's forces hailed them with a relentless bombardment. The determined Rose, however, kept pressing forward, despite casualties. This furious exchange of fire continued for about two hours. Then Rao Sahib's troops began to feel the heat and were forced to retreat to Lashkar.

It was an extremely anxious night. Lakshmibai, Tantya, Rao Sahib and the Nawab of Banda continued to discuss their strategy for the next day till the small hours of the morning.

When dawn broke, the Rani donned a red kurta and white churidar, the uniform of the men of the Gwalior contingent who were serving under her. She wrapped a white turban around her head, tucked her dagger into her waist and put on her pearl choker. Her beloved Sarangi had been killed at Golauli and she had replaced her with another fine steed, Rajratna. But the exertions of the last four days had worn the horse out, so she selected a fresh one. She embraced Damodar, praying that the day would go well and some happy times might be in store for them.

Lakshmibai rode out with her usual energy and determination to win. Her old friend Raghunath Singh would accompany her, as well as her dear Mandar.

It was 7 a.m. on 17 June, when Brigadier Smith arrived at the fort of Kotah-ki-Sarai with a sizeable force drawn from various regiments. He discovered that the rebels were waiting on a ridge about 1.5 km to the west, and made a quick decision. He first gave orders to store the supplies properly. Then he advanced towards his foes with a part of his troops—the horse-drawn artillery in front, followed by the infantry. Gul Muhammad was in charge of the artillery on the other side, and he met the British with an unrelenting barrage of fire. Smith had to retreat after a couple of volleys but pressed forward again. The battle swung back and forth. Both sides were determined not to give way. Eventually the British infantry prevailed and the Indian troops were compelled to back off. They headed towards Phoolbagh now.

When the British gave chase, Raghunath Singh attacked with his division, which was followed by an even larger contingent led by Lakshmibai herself, and Mandar. Now the British commanders, Raines and Vialls, were in serious trouble. Their troops were already suffering in the unbearable June heat, and this concerted assault dealt a severe blow to their sagging morale. The cries of 'Har-Har Mahadev!' struck terror into their hearts. The Rani led from the front, as usual, swinging out with her sword, cheering her soldiers on. She could see that the enemy was losing ground, and one determined push could win the day for them.

But the British had resources far beyond what the rebels could imagine. When the battle was going against them, Brigadier Smith sent in fresh reinforcements— the 8th Hussars under Captain Heneage. The tide of war turned again, despite the efforts of the gunners who kept up a relentless fire from the fort. Lakshmibai's army began to scatter, though she tried hard to organize a final stand. It is said that she struck out boldly with her sword, using both her hands, holding the reins of her horse in her mouth for greater ease of movement.

Soon she, Mandar and Raghunath Singh were cut off from the main force, along with just about a dozen men. The Hussars pursued them as they headed for Phoolbagh, realizing that this little group had great significance in the campaign. They did not know that Lakshmibai and Mandar were women—just that they were doughty warriors. According to one account, the Sonarekha stream lay before the queen as she urged her horse forward. The new steed baulked and just then Mandar cried out, 'I'm hit, Bai Sahiba! I'm gone!'

The Rani whirled around, struck out at Mandar's assailant and killed him. But she had barely dealt the deathblow when a sword slashed her head. She turned and forced her mount forward. When it finally managed to cross the stream, a bullet whizzed through the air to pierce her chest and she slumped on her horse.

Captain Heneage of the 8th Hussars, who witnessed it all, left an account of this fateful incident. It has been quoted in his brief biography *V.C. and D.S.O.* by O'Moore Creagh (V.C. stands for Victoria Cross; D.S.O. stands for Distinguished Service Order—both awards for gallantry). Note that the captain calls it 'his horse's neck', not knowing it was a woman:

> *There was no pretence of resistance any longer except from a slight, fully armed figure that was helplessly whirled along in this cataract of men and horses. Again and again this one leader, gesticulating and vociferating, attempted to stem the torrent of routed rebels, but all in vain. There was no possibility of holding up the broken Mahrattas, and at last a chance shot struck down across his horse's neck, this one champion of the retreating force. A moment later the swaying figure was overtaken, and one stroke from a Hussar's sabre ended the whole matter.*

Whether the bullet struck her first or the sword—the Rani had been mortally wounded. Gul Muhammad, Raghunath Singh and a couple more of her followers shot at her pursuers, killing one, while the others retreated. Then they dashed forward to search for the queen.

## Did the Rani actually die?

Many of the Rani's subjects in Jhansi refused to believe that she was dead, the way Subhas Chandra Bose's admirers continued to wait for him to return. Some British officers contributed to this legend, too, and several sightings were reported.

Even now people report that her ghost is sometimes glimpsed—on horseback on the Jhansi-Bhander road, or standing on the walls of the fort!

They found her horse roaming around restlessly. Lakshmibai still lay on its back, covered with blood. Gul Muhammad caught hold of its reins. They had to carry the queen to safety. The battle raged not too far from them and they all remembered the queen's words—that even her corpse should not be defiled by the touch of an Englishman.

They took her to the garden of Phoolbagh and discovered the hut of an ascetic, Baba Ganganath, close by. Gently, with tears streaming down their faces, they lowered the Rani on to a pile of straw that lay near the hut.

Life was fast ebbing away from her severely wounded frame. The best they could do to provide relief was to sponge her face with water from the stream. Damodar was hurriedly fetched. It is said that Ramchandra Deshmukh always carried a small container of Gangajal. He poured some between her lips, and her eyes flickered open briefly. 'Take care of Ananda,' she gasped, 'and distribute my ornaments among the troops.' Then she breathed her last, murmuring 'Har-Har Mahadev,' barely twenty minutes after she had been fatally injured.

Dusk was falling, but the queen's last rites had to be hurriedly performed. They could not afford to linger; the shouts, the hoof beats of the charging 8th Hussars already rang in their ears. The grieving party fled without even being able to perform the ceremony of removing her bones. Sir Robert Hamilton and others who reached the spot later found her ashes with pieces of bones still among them.

One of their most hated enemies was gone, and there was good reason for the British to rejoice. The rebel cause was in shambles without her inspiring leadership, though Rao Sahib and Tantya Tope continued the struggle till the latter was betrayed and captured in 1859. Rao Sahib evaded arrest till 1862. Both were hanged soon after they were caught.

The queen's beloved Damodar led the tortured life of a fugitive with her followers, Ramchandra Rao Deshmukh, Kashi and Raghunath Singh. They had to hide in the forests, constantly on the move, trying to evade the British soldiers who were scouring the countryside for them. Always delicate in health, Damodar was often ill, exposed to the elements as he was, with no way of knowing even where their next meal would come from. Little by little the money the queen had left vanished, grabbed by the greedy men to whom they had to turn for help. When all her jewellery was gone, Raghunath Singh, with the support of the Raja of Patan, Prithvi Singh, approached the British agent at Indore, Sir Richmond Shakespeare, who arranged for a pension for Damodar's upkeep.

With the support of this meagre pension, Damodar led a modest life in Indore. Despite all his efforts, he never received his true inheritance, which the British government claimed to be holding in trust for him.

Lakshmibai left the world like a true patriot and warrior, fighting for her motherland. Many, who refused to accept that she was dead, said that she had been carried away, and the corpse that had been burned was Mandar's. However conflicting the accounts of her final hours may be, the Rani soon became a legend. She lived on in the folk songs that were sung by bards, countless tales told of her exploits and numerous books written on her life, both biographies and novels in different languages, Indian and foreign. She became one of the most enduring icons of the freedom struggle against British rule, and till date remains a source of inspiration for women's empowerment.

A small monument at Gwalior marks the spot where she was cremated. It lies in front of the imposing Phoolbagh palace. An inscription reads: *This monument marks the site of the cremation of the illustrious and heroic Maharani Luxmi Bai of Jhansi, who fell in a battle in the Sepoy War of 1857–58.*

While many of the British reviled her as the 'Jezebel of India', her more than worthy opponent Hugh Rose acknowledged her great qualities. When he wrote his version of the campaign, he said: 'Although a lady, she was the bravest and best military leader of the rebels. A man among the mutineers.'

The Rani was much more than that. She was a woman far ahead of her times, one who was bold enough to stand up for what she believed in, against the mightiest power of her era. This is the reason why she still remains a much admired role model and one of most fascinating heroes of the freedom struggle. As Jawaharlal Nehru wrote: 'One name stands out above others and is still revered in popular memory, the name of Lakshmi Bai, Rani of Jhansi.' Thus, she remains immortal, vindicating what her followers passionately believed—that the brave Rani could never die.

### Left motherless . . .

Damodar Rao's loss was perhaps the greatest. True, his biological mother was still alive. It is said that she came to meet him after Lakshmibai's death, while he was living in Indore. But they were unable to bond and she had to return, disappointed. He was too attached to the Rani to accept even his real mother in her place.

# TRIVIA
# TREASURY

Turn the pages to discover more fascinating facts and tantalizing tidbits of history about this legendary life and her world.

# WHAT HAPPENED AND WHEN

- **1770:** Raghunath Hari Newalkar is appointed subedar of Jhansi by Peshwa Bajirao I.
- **1804:** The East India Company acknowledges his successor, Shivrao Bhau, as an independent ruler of Jhansi.
- **1818:** Peshwa Bajirao II is banished to Bithur; his brother Chimnaji Appa settles in Varanasi. Moropant's father Balwant Rao accompanies him.
- **1827:** Manikarnika is born to Moropant Tambe and Bhagirathibai in Varanasi.
- **1829:** Bhagirathibai passes away.
- **1832:** Chimnaji Appa dies and Moropant moves to Bithur.
- **1838:** British appoint Gangadhar Rao as ruler of Jhansi.
- **1842:** Gangadhar Rao marries Manikarnika, who is renamed Lakshmibai.
- **1851:** A son, Damodar Rao, is born to Lakshmibai but dies three months later.
- **1853:** Gangadhar Rao dies after adopting Ananda Rao, who is renamed Damodar Rao.

- **1854:** Lord Dalhousie refuses to recognize the adoption and applies the Doctrine of Lapse. He annexes Jhansi, and British administration is established.
- **1857:** Sepoys rebel against British rule in several parts of northern India.
- **June 1857:** British residents are killed by Indian troops in Jhansi. Lakshmibai takes over reins of government.
- **September 1857:** British reoccupy Delhi and banish Mughal Emperor Bahadur Shah Zafar.
- **November 1857:** Lucknow is conquered by the British.
- **January 1858:** Sir Hugh Rose leaves Mhow and heads towards Jhansi.
- **March 1858:** Rose reaches Jhansi after fighting several battles on the way.
- **April 1858:** Jhansi falls after a heroic defence. Rani escapes to Kalpi and joins up with Rao Sahib and Tantya Tope.
- **May 1858:** The combined forces of Rani Lakshmibai, Rao Sahib, Tantya Tope and their allies are defeated by Rose at Krunch and later Golauli near Kalpi.
- **1 June 1858:** Rani Lakshmibai and her allies take over Gwalior.
- **17 June 1858:** Hugh Rose attacks Gwalior and the Rani dies fighting.
- **August 1858:** East India Company's rule ends; the British Crown takes over.
- **1859:** Tantya Tope is captured and executed.
- **1862:** Rao Sahib is captured and executed.

# 1857 AND THE WORLD

1857 was an eventful year, full of landmarks.

- **9 January:** An earthquake with an estimated magnitude of 7.9 strikes near Parkfield, California, with only two fatalities.
- **24 January:** University of Calcutta opens in Kolkata as the first multi-disciplinary modern university in South Asia. University of Mumbai also founded the same year.
- **22 February:** Robert Baden-Powell, English founder of the Scout movement, born in Paddington, England.
- **3 March:** France and the United Kingdom formally declare war on China in the Second Opium War.
- **4 March:** James Buchanan succeeds Franklin Pierce as US President.
- **6 March:** Landmark case, Dred Scott vs. Stanford. The Supreme Court of the United States rules that Blacks are not citizens and slaves cannot sue for freedom, driving the country closer to the American Civil War.
- **21 March:** An earthquake in Tokyo, Japan, kills over 1,00,000.
- **23 March:** Elisha Otis' first elevator is installed in 488 Broadway, New York City.
- **13 May:** Ronald Ross, who discovered the malaria parasite, born in Almora, India.

- **13 September:** Milton S. Hershey, American chocolate manufacturer, born in Derry Church, Pennsylvania.
- **13 October:** New York banks close following a major financial panic and do not reopen until 12 December.
- **24 October:** Sheffield F.C., the world's first association football team, launched in Sheffield, England.
- **3 December:** Joseph Conrad, famous Polish-British novelist, born in Berdychiv, now in the Ukraine.
- **16 December:** An earthquake with an estimated magnitude of 6.9 kills 11,000 people in Naples, Italy.

# OTHER REBELLIONS AGAINST BRITISH RULE

The 1857 uprising was not the first rebellion against British rule. Several others occurred before it and soon after, or were still continuing when it occurred.

- **Sanyasi and Fakir Uprisings in Bengal (1770)**

A sect of sanyasis rose against the British during and after the great Bengal famine of 1770. Led by Majnu Shah and Cheragh Ali, a large number of fakirs or Muslim mendicants also revolted against the British around the same time.

- **Faraizi Movement (1804–1860)**

Haji Shariatullah of Faridpur (eastern Bengal) launched this movement in 1804 to remove unIslamic practices from Muslim society and restore Muslim rule by expelling the Christian British from India. His successors Dudu Mian and Nowa Mian mobilized Muslim peasants against the mostly Hindu zamindars, moneylenders and the British indigo planters. The Bengal government was finally able to suppress it in 1860.

- **Wahabi Movement (1820–1870)**

Originally an Islamic socio-religious reform movement, it was also meant to purify Islam. Saiyad Ahmad of Rae Bareilly was its founder in India. He aimed to restore Muslim rule by overthrowing the Sikhs in Punjab and the British in Bengal. Wahabism spread very rapidly in Bihar, Bengal, UP and north-western India. The British took strong measures and were able to eradicate it completely around 1870.

- **The Kuka Movement in the Punjab (1860–1872)**

Bhagat Jawahar Mal began this movement in 1840 to reform the Sikh religion by getting rid of superstitions and wrong practices. After the British annexed Punjab, restoration of Sikh sovereignty became its major objective. The British were able to put it down by 1872.

- **The Santhal Rebellion (1855–1856)**

Led by Sidhu and Kanhu, thousands of Santhals revolted against the tyranny of the British and their local Indian collaborators. They attacked landlords, moneylenders, planters and British officials, and proclaimed the end of British rule. The British found it hard to subdue this rebellion, and accomplished it only when the army was called in.

# THE EAST INDIA COMPANY

- In 1600, the East India Company was launched as a commercial venture when Queen Elizabeth I granted the group a charter to trade with the East Indies (now Indonesia).

- Their ships arrived in India, docking at Surat, which was established as a trade transit point in 1608. Within the next two years, the Company shifted its major operations to India and built its first factory in Machilipatnam on the Coromandel coast.

- In 1615, instructed by James I, Sir Thomas Roe visited the Mughal Emperor Jahangir to negotiate a commercial treaty granting the Company the exclusive rights to reside and build factories in Surat and other areas. In return, the Company offered to provide the emperor with goods and rarities from the European market. Soon it had factories and trading posts in many parts of the country, arousing resentment among local rulers.

- In 1757, Robert Clive defeated Siraj-ud-daulah, the Nawab of Bengal, at the Battle of Plassey. The Company acquired a strong foothold and, with the Mughal empire crumbling, continued its territorial acquisitions, which spread all over India.

- In 1858, the British government ended the Company rule after the tumultuous war of 1857 and took over.

- The East India Company was also described as 'John Company' and 'Company Bahadur'.

## LAKSHMIBAI LIVES ON ...

The Bundelas may have been right when they said Lakshmibai will live on forever. Perhaps there's hardly a city in India that does not possess a road, an institution, a public building or park named after her. Her statues, usually equestrian ones, can be found across Indian cities, from Jhansi to Gwalior and Pune to Ahmedabad. Stories, songs, plays, films and stamps, all keep her memory alive.

- *Jhansi ki Rani* released in 1952 was the first Indian film to be shot entirely in Technicolor. Sohrab Modi directed it, and popular actress Mehtab played the title role. A dubbed version was released in the U.S.A. in 1956 under the title *Tiger and the Flame*. It also travelled to West Germany. Recently many other projects have been announced with actresses ranging from Aishwarya Rai, Sushmita Sen to Deepika Padukone taking on the Rani's role.

- On 15 August 1957, the Government of India issued a stamp bearing the figure of the Rani of Jhansi to celebrate the first centenary of the War of 1857.

- Many awards carry Lakshmibai's name, like the Stree Shakti Puraskar awarded by the Centre, the Uttar Pradesh Sports Award for women and various others.

- Her bravery has passed into popular speech—when people talk about a gutsy woman, they describe her as a 'Jhansi ki Rani'.

# BOOKS TO READ

Here are some books you can read if you wish to find out more about Rani Lakshmibai and the 1857 War of Independence:

1. *A Flight of Pigeons* by Ruskin Bond (Penguin Books India, 2002; originally published 1975)
2. *The Last Mughal* by William Dalrymple (Penguin/Viking, 2006)
3. *Rani Lakshmibai: The Indian Heroine* by Shahana Dasgupta (Rupa & Co., 2002)
4. *The Queen of Jhansi* by Mahashweta Devi, trs. Mandira and Sagaree Sengupta (Seagull Books, 2000)
5. *The Rani of Jhansi: Rebel against Will* by Rainer Jerosch, trs. James. A. Turner (Peter Lang Ltd, Frankfurt am Main, 2003; this edition, Aakar Books, 2007)
6. *Folk Songs on 1857* by P.C. Joshi, ed. (National Book Trust, 2007)
7. *Rani of Jhansi Lakshmi Bai* by Paul, E. Jaiwant (Roli Books, 1997)
8. *Eighteen Fifty-Seven* by S.N. Sen (Publications Division, Ministry of Information and Broadcasting, Government of India, 1957)
9. *The Rebellious Rani* by Sir John Smyth VC, MC (Frederick Muller Ltd, 1966)
10. *Jhansi ki Rani Lakshmibai* by Vrindavan Lal Verma (Prabhat Prakashan, 1993)

You will also find lots more about the Rani and the 1857 War of Independence on several websites; all you have to do is Google.

# Other Books in the Series

## *Jawaharlal Nehru: The Jewel of India*
### *By Aditi De*

**At midnight on 14 August 1947, Jawaharlal Nehru rose to speak to independent India as its first Prime Minister. He was dressed in a pale cream *achkan*, a white khadi cap on his head. Though his eyes had shadows beneath them, they grew brighter as Jawaharlal began to speak . . .**

Pandit Nehru's words that night have remained etched in the nation's memory ever since. Born to a privileged family in Allahabad, Jawaharlal went on to become a leading figure of the Indian independence movement. During the struggle he spent over ten years in prison, watched others in his family jailed time and again, and led numerous protest marches and agitations. Working alongside Mahatma Gandhi, he helped India keep its tryst with destiny and become a free nation.

Aditi De recounts the story of Jawaharlal Nehru's extraordinary life in this sparkling biography for young readers. Filled with charming anecdotes, it recounts episodes from Nehru's childhood, and how he was drawn to the growing struggle for Indian independence. She sketches his role as the first Indian Prime Minister, and how he shaped the newly-formed democratic republic. Packed with little-known nuggets of information, and trivia about the times, this book in the *Puffin Lives* series brings alive the thoughts and actions of one of modern India's most important personalities.

# Other Books in the Series

## Ashoka: The Great and Compassionate King
### By Subhadra Sen Gupta

**After the fierce battle of Kalinga, the victorious king stood in the middle of the terrible carnage he had wrought, in a battlefield filled with the dead and dying, and took a close look at what he had achieved . . .**

The transformation that came over this king after one of his most significant victories at war made him into a legend forever. Ashoka the Great, the ruler of ancient India's largest kingdom, took the path of peace, tolerance, non-violence and compassion. He now addressed his subjects as a father would his children, and erected pillars that spread his thoughts throughout the land in the people's own language. He put their welfare above all else and worked towards that for the rest of his life. One of the most well-known symbols from India's history, the Ashoka chakra, now adorns India's national flag, and the lion capital from his pillars is our national emblem.

In this lively, engrossing account of Ashoka's life and the times, Subhadra Sen Gupta deftly brings him alive again from behind the swirling mists of time. It is a story about war, devotion and a king's love for his people, embellished with many details about Mauryan society, battle codes and even freaky food facts! Plunge into some of the most dramatic episodes of India's history with the *Puffin Lives* series and let the past speak to you like never before.